HOW TO
Change
YOUR
HUSBAND
IN 30 DAYS

RHONDA C. WHITE

Copyright © 2022 by Rhonda C. White

ISBN: 978-1-943342-44-0

Unless otherwise noted, all Scripture references are from the King James Version. All rights reserved.

How To Change Your Husband in 30 Days

Rhonda C. White
thedaddyvoidproject@gmail.com

Destined To Publish
Flossmoor, Illinois
www.DestinedToPublish.com

INTRODUCTION

Okay, I've got your attention, right? What wife wouldn't want change for or in her husband? Even the good ones need some help too, right? A little tuck here or a little nip there wouldn't hurt, huh? What about those dreams you had regarding marriage and your Knight in Shining Armor? Have you done anything with those expectations? Are they still attainable? You know, those things that you were sure your husband was going to do or say or be before you got married because he loved you?

Those things that were going to change about him once he said "I do," because he was saying "I do" to you! You remember those things that used to be so cute? Those same things that have now turned into a pain in your you-know-what? Have your dreams of riding off into the sunset with Mr. Right faded into what seems like a dream that did not come true?

Well, look no further, my friend, because this is the challenge for you! It has your name written all over it. Too often in marriage, we come to a decision that things are just not what they should be, and slowly we take a path which ultimately ends up in a lonely marriage, a separation (physical or emotional), or even divorce. We either decide to retaliate or internalize our emotions, since our prayers of "Change him, Lord" go unanswered year after year. As a result, we become less involved and less in love with our husbands. The divorce rate is skyrocketing, especially in the homes of those who claim to be believers. Apparently, believers who know better have learned what the Lord says about marriage, but have failed miserably at applying what He says.

Unfortunately, sometimes as wives, we give up way too easily, and all the appropriate praying and fasting that we've done for our husbands ends up benefiting his next woman in line, and in some cases the next man! Our giving up sometimes shows a refusal to give God the amount of time He desires to make the difference. Many of us feel that if our husband would just do "_____," things would be okay. However, even in many cases when that "blank" is filled, wives still find themselves disjointed and disappointed about the state of their marriages, because they were not ready for the blessing and essentially messed over or overlooked what God did in their spouses.

Well, it is time for a change, and I pray that you will believe God with me to heal and restore your marriage in His way and in His timing. Every marriage needs healing! Even if you are in a good place right now, store up the healing for when you are not. All marriages go through seasons, and unfortunately there is inclement weather associated with each one. The best marriages just learn how to prepare and withstand the storms to survive.

PAUSE! TAKE A BREATH AND THEN KEEP READING, BECAUSE WE ARE ABOUT TO MAKE A TURN AND I WANT YOU TO BRACE FOR IT!!

If you haven't caught on by now, the changes you can dramatically expect to occur after reading and applying the spiritual principles in this challenge do not have much to do with getting your husband told or leaving him little messages in the bathroom about what he needs to improve. This guide will not even encourage you to give his best friends a call to ask them to talk to him about how he is driving you crazy. And no, this book is not a lesson on how to tell his momma how much she did to make your husband the way he is!

No, this challenge is designed especially for wives who are tired of expecting changes to occur in their marriages because they scream, fight, and roll on the floor, believing that one day things will get better, just because. Don't worry, I'm not talking about you unless the shoe fits. And if it does fit, tie it up and let's get moving. I am right here with you, and I have the shoes on too!

This challenge was created with the woman in mind who desires spiritual maturity and want to see the benefits of it in her marriage. The woman who refuses to believe that her husband is all bad and understands that some of the issues in their marriage might have a little to do with her. Even if you don't think that's you, even if your faith is shattered and your belief system is shaken, I encourage you to consider this challenge, because I want you to know that God's Word has a proven track record. Can I lend you enough of my faith for you to at least try it out? The truth is the truth whether or not we know it or accept it. *God's Word guarantees us that we can have the joy of the Lord in our lives and marriages, despite the trials that we face, if we only trust His timing and apply His principles.*

I admonish and challenge you to believe God for the next 30 days. If you allow Him to minister to you through your commitment to His Word by completing this guide, *God will do the miraculous!* The change, however, begins with you! The change must occur in you first, and then everything else that is out of order in your life will have to follow suit. Change occurs with one movement, one effort, just one try. It is all a part of God's perfect law. He will mold the one who is most available and willing so that the metamorphoses can resurrect the dead, save the lost, and set the captives free.

Why not give God's way a chance? Haven't you been doing it your way long enough? Are you happy with the results? Even if your marriage is not headed for divorce court, couldn't it benefit from having a wife who is sold out to God's principles regarding marriage? If you want to continue to live in insanity (*"insanity" means to continue to do the same thing repeatedly and expect different results*) then pass this challenge on; it is not for you. Some wife or future wife is waiting for you to share it with her instead. But if you are ready to see the blessings of the Lord flow through you to your marriage, and to see things in your life and in your husband's life change for the better, then stand with me and God for the next 30 days and complete this challenge.

Please pray the following:

Lord,

I recognize that You have called me to be a wife. Marriage is a part of your perfect plan for my life. I recognize Your power and Your ability to work through me when I am submissive to Your will. I accept the challenge that You have given me, and for the next 30 days, I will submit to Your will regarding my marriage and not my own.

I believe Your Word works, and I am tired of not believing it long enough to see the manifestation of miracles that it promises. Change me, Lord, into the forgiving, obedient, trusting, and submissive servant in my marriage that You designed me to be.

In Jesus' name,

Amen.

Now write the following statement out and post it somewhere you can see daily.

I _____ commit the next 30 days to believing God for a manifestation of blessings to flow through me to my marriage. I will not contemplate quitting or giving up until I see my change come. I realize that I determine the climate in my home, and because of my transformation, it will be a place of peace and restoration, and I will become a change agent for my husband.

_____   _____
Signature   Date

CHALLENGE, REVIEW AND OUTLINE

It has been said that it takes 21 days to make or break a habit, and this challenge has been designed with that principle in mind. Anything that can be implemented in 21 days can surely be ingrained in the heart of a believer in 30 days. As you embark on this challenge, you will be led to explore six areas of your walk as a wife. You will be asked to revisit (or visit for the first time) forgiveness, obedience, trust, submission, consistency, and commitment as it relates to your marriage and your husband.

Each area of discussion can either be an assist or an impediment to your success in being the wife God desires you to be, depending on how well you embrace each individual calling. That's correct! A godly wife is called to a live a life of forgiveness, obedience, trust, submission, consistency, and commitment. Without her desire and true dedication to being successful in every area, her marriage is bound to suffer consequences that could potentially have been avoided with the execution of those principles.

Let's take a closer look at why each area is vital to the life of every successful wife.

Forgiveness: Our entire faith as believers is based on the principle of forgiveness. In a nutshell, forgiveness is a refusal to hold oneself or another accountable for injustices performed knowingly or unknowingly. In marriage, forgiveness is something that needs to occur on a continual basis. Just as Christianity doesn't work if God does not forgive us, a marriage can't function without the art of forgiveness. This guide begins by focusing for seven days on the need to forgive self and others, including our husbands.

Obedience: This nine-letter word has silently killed many marriages due to not understanding how it applies in a marriage and misusing the power attached to it. Obedience simply means to comply with or hold in high regard a figure of authority. God designed a hierarchy in every institution He created. He did not create it to suppress its subordinates, but to protect them. Obedience to God and to the authority that He has placed over us in marriage brings forth life and peace. Seven days of this challenge focus on the need to be obedient to God's will to prevent the congestion or blocking of blessings of peace and prosperity.

Trust: So many times, our circumstances inhibit us from trusting God and our spouses with the delicate parts of our lives. Due to hurt and pain, we decide to guard and protect our emotions as a defense against what has happened in the past. Although this defense is natural and in theory should prove to be a benefit, it truly only wrecks the vitality and sucks the oxygen out of any marriage. Without the ability to have faith in God and to rely solely on Him regarding our husbands, not on the chronicles we keep on them, we walk the destiny of our own marriages down a road of doom and destruction. Seven days of the challenge are devoted to learning how to trust God and His timing, which will subsequently teach us to trust our spouses.

Submission: Aahhh! Did someone say "Mufasa?" Just like in the movie *The Lion King*, the sound of the word "submission" can freeze and silence crowds. Submission is daunting, especially when the world screams at us that it will bring us harm and not good. A submissive wife is one who willingly remains in a state of acquiescence to the power and authority given to her husband by God. She does not allow this state to cause her to sin, but instead finds protection and peace in her ability to maintain her position in the covenant she made to God when she entered marriage. This guide reviews submission for seven days to ensure that you can master a complete surrender to the practice of submission in your marriage.

Consistency: One day is solely dedicated to training and disciplining you in how to be constant, steady, reliable, even, regular, and stable in your ability to walk in forgiveness, obedience, trust, and submission, even when what you see says not to, and even when it hurts. Consistency will be addressed throughout the guide with each individual discussion but will be the central focus of this one day.

Commitment: The promise and vow to achieve excellence in each of the aforementioned topics will be reviewed daily. The last day of this challenge looks at commitment more closely as a refresher and as a catalyst for integrating the learned principles in hopes of providing a sustaining power for any wife who dares to commit to the 30-day challenge.

Guide Outline: Each day has a daily affirmation regarding our aim, a memory verse, helpful hints for maintaining the course of action, advice about "what to do when you fail," and journal space to respond to a daily "heart question" and write a reflection on that day's topic.

Daily affirmation: To be repeated several times throughout the day as a reminder of the daily focus point.

Memory verse: A scripture pertaining to the topic, to be learned and reviewed throughout the day and over the course of the 30 days as needed.

Helpful hints: This area will add validity to the importance of the topic regarding the role of a wife. This is the nourishment for the challenge. It should be reviewed as many times as needed throughout the day. It is a source of practical application.

"What to do when you fail": This is the "plan of action" section that should be used in the event you fall off course and need to get back on track. You do not need to quit the challenge when you fail... Just get back up and start over again. Tomorrow is coming! Change is coming!

Heart question: These questions will give you an opportunity to ask yourself honest questions regarding the topic.

Reflection: In this section, you will gather your thoughts about the topic, helping to personalize your journey.

*Note to the reader: God guarantees results with the use of His Word. If He did not, we would be able to call Him a liar, and He will not allow that. Your breakthroughs may not come as fast as you would like, simply because God does not run on our schedules; we run on His. The trials you are facing right now in your marriage have brought you to the exact place where God wants you. The trial could be for correction, discipline, sanctification, or preparation for the next level. He uses everything to bring you closer to Him and to bring glory to His name. You may find that you need to repeat this challenge several times until it becomes your lifestyle, but once you have done what God says, there is no way He will not be faithful and do what He promises. Your life will be changed, your marriage will be changed, and ultimately your spouse will be changed. May God bless you on your journey. His blessings are waiting on the other side of the next 30 days.

ADDITIONAL TIDBITS

- Begin praying at least 3-5 days prior to starting the challenge for wisdom, deliverance, and endurance. God is ready for you to succeed, but the enemy and the world want you to fail because you are not succeeding their way. The more girded up you are, the more prepared and successful you will be.

- The daily devotions for this challenge should be read first thing in the morning so that you have the full day for application. You will need at most 30 minutes to complete your devotion/journaling for the day.

- This challenge is best performed with a partner or a buddy. It is important to have someone you can be accountable to during your journey. Even if you decide to go it alone, tell someone you trust (other than your husband) so that they can keep tabs on you.

- It is also wise to cut out as many outside distractions as possible during this journey. For example, the television and secular radio programming often project subtle or not-so-subtle negative images of marriage and worldly opinions about how to handle difficult situations. These outside opinions will clutter your mind and make the challenge more difficult. Minimizing internet use and idle chatter will help to produce more positive results as well. If need be, let your friends know what you are doing. You don't want to be rude and legalistic with your challenge, but you can't expect to change if you don't change!

- Another good idea is to monitor what you are eating and drinking during this time. The next 30 days is a time of discipline and growth. When we put unhealthy substances in our body, we only impede our ability to concentrate and respond positively to daily circumstances. Our emotional well-being is directly connected to our physical well-being. Eat healthy, well-balanced meals and drink plenty of water (at least half your body weight in ounces each day).

- Make sure you get enough rest and exercise during this 30-day period as well. A rested mind and energized body will do wonders for your ability to hear from God and be obedient to His call.

- This challenge will not be successful unless it is bathed in prayer. If you are not a woman of prayer, you need to become one first. I challenge you to double the amount of prayer time you have now. If you have set aside time once a day for prayer, make it twice. I also encourage you to slather your day with one to two-sentence prayers to keep you focused on the day's mission.

- God wants you to have a "root revelation" during this 30-day challenge. This means that on this journey, He wants you to dig deep, down where the root of your marriage issues lies. Think about an onion: when we are cooking with an onion, we often start by pulling off the layers. In the work of marriage, we do the same thing. We spend time trying to pull the layers off. Sometimes we get to a slick layer, and sometimes we come to a rough one. All things said, we struggle, our hands get stinky, and our eyes water, but we never reach the heart of the matter if we don't pull off enough layers. This is because we are dealing with the object and not its root.

The true issues in our marriage lie at the very root of it, at its core. You will never be able to experience God the way He intended until you dissect the root and encounter the revelation that lies there. We cut off the roots of our produce and don't want to think about them because they are in the ugly, cold, wet, dark dirt of our past. It's not fun getting your hands messy, getting dirt under your nails, but again, that is where the real revelations lie. (Revelations are enlightening or astonishing disclosures.) Are you ready to experience the true identity of your marriage? Are you ready to let God work from the inside out so that He can reproduce the good and the great that He has for you and your husband?

- During this challenge you will need a few items in order to complete the daily tasks and challenges. Get access to them now so that you are ready
    — a small journal
    — a rubber band
    — paper/pen
    — small package clay or playdough
    — timer/stopwatch
    — small photocopy of a lamb

"A wife of noble character who can find? She is worth far more than rubies. Her husband has full confidence in her and lacks nothing of value. She brings him good, not harm, all the days of her life." Proverbs 31:10–12 NIV

LET THE GAMES BEGIN....

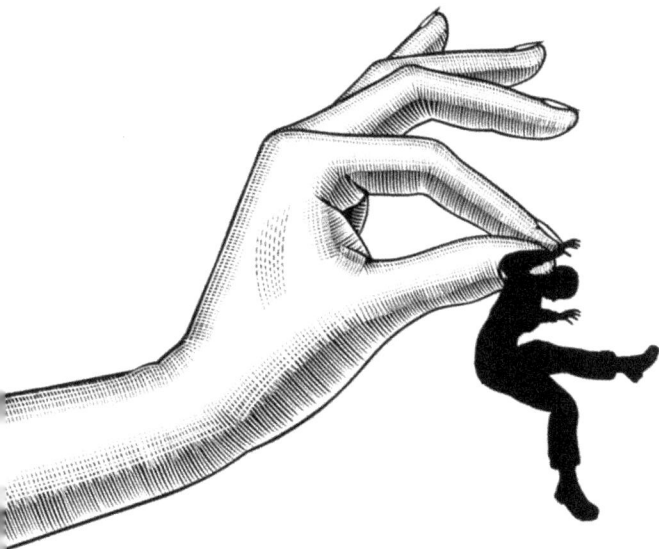

FORGIVENESS (DAY 1)

/fər giv'nis/ *The act of granting free pardon or remission for an offense*

DAILY AFFIRMATION: "I will walk in forgiveness of self today."

MEMORY VERSE: *"There is therefore now no condemnation to them which are in Christ Jesus, who walk not after the flesh, but after the Spirit."* **Romans 8:1** KJV

HELPFUL HINTS: Believers begin their journey with God with forgiveness. We cannot accept Christ as our Savior without the gift of His forgiveness. Forgiveness must be a path that we consciously choose as believers. If we do not, our walk is destined to veer off its predestined path. We can never truly forgive others if we let our own failures, mistakes, and sins stagnate

the flow of God's love toward us. (See the section on salvation at the end of this book if you have questions about becoming a believer.)

Forgiveness is a state of the heart, and it must start within us. Decide today to quit making excuses about the things you've done. Yeah, you were late yesterday, yeah, you didn't respond to your husband like you should have, but it is over. Yesterday is gone, and your worries and concerns about it should be gone too. There is nothing you can do but decide to love yourself anyway. We all make mistakes; get over it and get on to accepting God's unconditional love for you. Guess what: He knew you were going to do it anyway, and yet He still loves you. Your forgiveness of yourself is not a charge card to sin, but a vehicle to move forward to bigger and better things. Make it a habit today and for the rest of your life to forgive yourself immediately, correct what you can, and move forward.

Jesus is saying to you today, "Go on with your day, I still love you regardless! Oh, and you are forgiven!"

"WHAT TO DO" IF YOU FAIL: Forgiveness is a state of mind, not a natural act. It takes training and discipline. Place a rubber band around your wrist, and when you find yourself walking in a state of blame or condemnation over something you did not do quite right, give yourself a snap on the wrist as a reminder that if God is able to forgive you, you can too! Say "ouch!" Laugh, and let it go!

💜 **HEART QUESTION:** List one thing for which you have refused to forgive yourself for up to this point and, as a result, continually walk in shame and self-blame.

_____

_____

_____

_____

_____

REFLECTION: Use the space below to ponder on why God thought enough of you to forgive you for the above sin or failure. Describe how your lack of self-forgiveness has affected you as a wife. Practice forgiveness of self all day until it becomes a natural process.

_____

_____

_____

_____

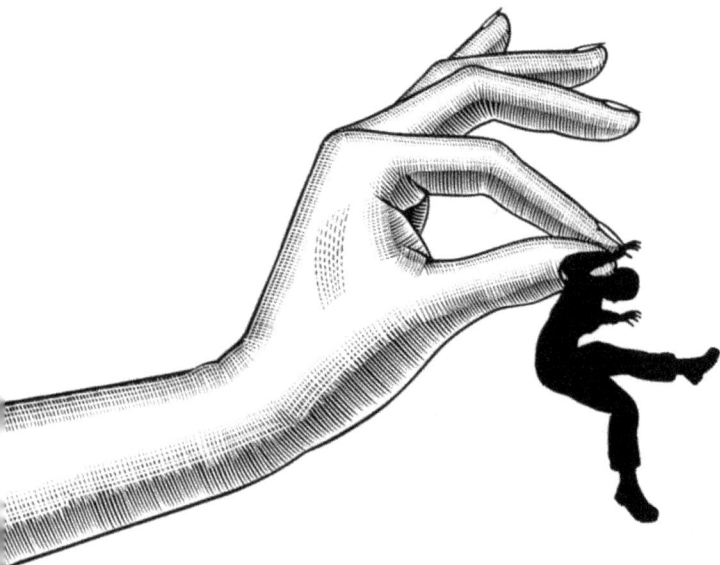

FORGIVENESS (DAY 2)

/fər giv'nis/ *The act of granting free pardon or remission for an offense*

DAILY AFFIRMATION: "I will walk in forgiveness of others today."

MEMORY VERSE: *"For if you forgive men when they sin against you, your heavenly Father will also forgive you. But if you do not forgive men their sins, your Father will not forgive your sins."* **Matthew 6:14-15** KJV

HELPFUL HINTS: We all have wounds from the past that continue to haunt us in the present and still will in our future if we let them go unchecked. These pains are real and devastating. One woman may be dealing with the abandonment of her biological father, while the next one is dealing with the wounds from a rape.

Others may have had a falling out with a childhood friend or been betrayed by a co-worker. The fact is, God knew we would be wounded by our circumstances, but He did not intend for us *not* to recover from them. In God's eyes all things, including pain, work together for good (Romans 8:28).

When you first hear that, it sounds foreign and even cruel. How could a God of love use pain for my good? We must learn to lay our history books of pain on the altar before the Lord so that He can close them. When we have a willing heart to forgive, God can implement His plan of judgment on our offenders. If we are in the way, He won't move. God forbid you be in His line of fire when He acts on "Vengeance is mine, saith the Lord" (Deuteronomy 32:35; Romans 12:19)! Recognize today that you were wronged, but that God will give you beauty for ashes when you follow His plan. Let it go today! That person has gone on with their life and left you defeated spiritually. You are more than a conqueror today! You can make the choice to forgive. As many times as you need to today, rehearse the act of forgiveness until you feel a release in your consciousness.

"WHAT TO DO" IF YOU FAIL: Continue to use your rubber band today when you need to forgive yourself, but as a way of release, write a letter to a person you need to forgive from your past, and explain what you are doing and why. You may or may not

be able to mail the letter, but it will give you an opportunity to begin the process of forgiving others. You will feel an emotional release from just getting your thoughts out on paper.

💜 **HEART QUESTION:** How have I set up barriers in my life to prevent others from hurting me again? Have these barriers been helpful in my growth as a believer?

_____

_____

_____

_____

_____

_____

_____

_____

_____

_____

_____

_____

REFLECTION: Use the space below to write a plan of action for how you will respond the next time someone requires forgiveness from you. List each step and make sure they are achievable. Regarding forgiving others, refer to this section as often as you need to, or least until you have memorized your steps and are able to implement them without review.

_____

_____

_____

_____

_____

_____

_____

_____

_____

_____

_____

_____

_____

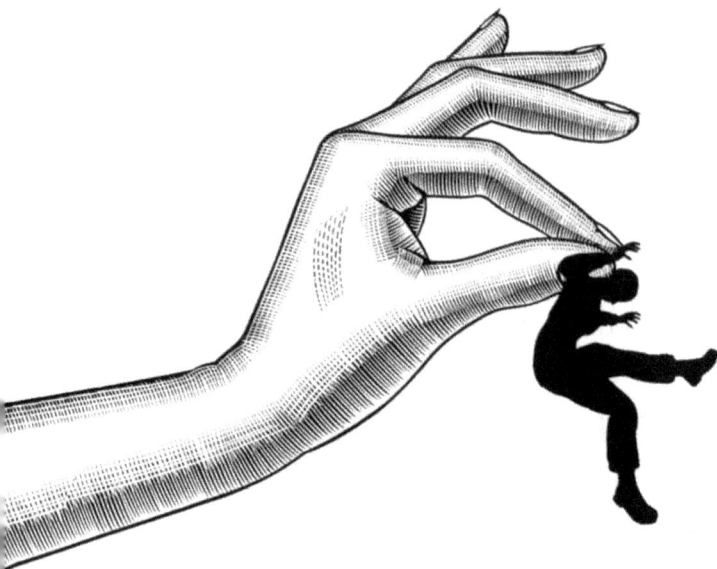

FORGIVENESS (DAY 3)

/fər giv'nis/ *The act of granting free pardon or remission for an offense*

DAILY AFFIRMATION: "I will walk in forgiveness of my husband's past offenses today."

MEMORY VERSE: *"Above all, love each other deeply, because love covers over a multitude of sins."* **1 Peter 4:8** NIV

HELPFUL HINTS: "Wahhh!" I hear your hearts screaming right now. "If I forgive all my husband's past offenses, what will fuel my anger toward him when I really need it?" Ladies, we are masters of the replay. We can bring back emotions from what our husbands did 15 years ago! Even though it seems that replaying all the pain will do us some good, in the end, all it does is stir up fresh heartache, resentment, and unforgiveness.

God did not intend for us to be record-keepers. When we sin, God places our sins in the sea of forgetfulness (Micah 7:19), but as wives, we have been known to be deep-sea divers! Yes, he was wrong, but how is holding onto it making you a better wife? God will never be able to heal the brokenness in your life if you continue to put your own band-aids on it.

Forgiveness has miraculous power! Holding on to something that does not belong to you eventually causes determent to your soul. God says His burdens are easy and His yoke is light (Matthew 11:30.) Forgiveness may sound hard, but it is as easy as handing your car keys over to someone else. It is a conscious act. When we allow our husbands to make mistakes and refuse to hold them accountable to being perfect, God can then heal us in every area. When we commit to stopping the nonsense of being "Holy Ghost juniors" for our spouses and allow the conviction of the Lord to change the fabric of their lives, we begin to see change. Let forgiveness seep in and out of your pores today. God can bathe you in forgiveness for your husband. Allow grace and mercy to clothe you so that when those past hurts surface, you are protected from them. Practice your plan of forgiveness consciously today, and allow your spouse to be the first one to benefit from it.

"WHAT TO DO" IF YOU FAIL: Every time you are reminded of your husband's past offenses, remind yourself of one great thing that your husband does consistently. Pray the floodgates open to him performing that act repeatedly because of your forgiveness of his past transgressions toward you. Snap that rubber band if your thoughts wander off into the deep end. Snap back into reality, girlfriend! Forgiveness can work if you work it.

HEART QUESTION: What is the real reason why I hold on to what my husband has done wrong to me? How does holding on to the pain benefit my marriage?

_____

_____

_____

_____

_____

_____

_____

_____

REFLECTION: List five benefits that you might receive if you honestly forgave your husband. Now imagine yourself being granted those things for a moment. If that life is better than the one you have now, what's stopping you from getting there?

_____

_____

_____

_____

_____

_____

_____

_____

_____

_____

_____

_____

_____

_____

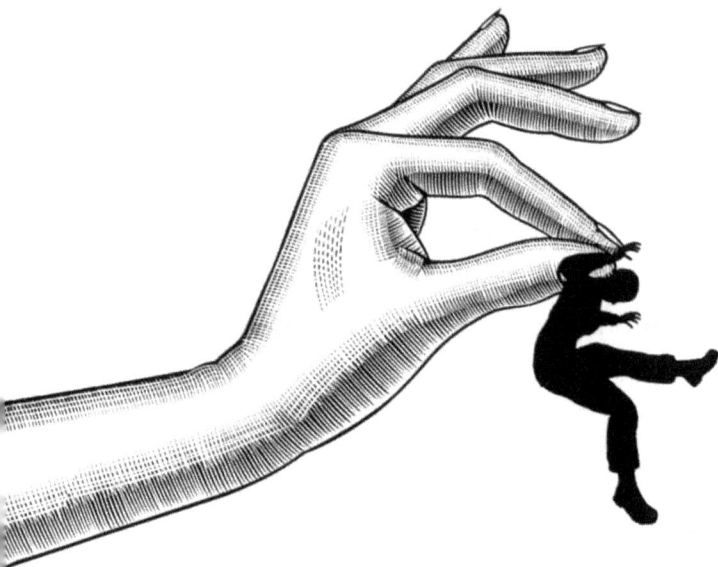

FORGIVENESS (DAY 4)

/fər giv'nis/ *The act of granting free pardon or remission for an offense*

DAILY AFFIRMATION: "I will walk in forgiveness of my husband's current offenses today."

MEMORY VERSE: *"Humble yourselves, therefore, under God's mighty hand, that he may lift you up in due time. Cast all your anxiety on him because he cares for you."* **1 Peter 5:6-7** NIV

HELPFUL HINTS: Wow! What burdens could be lifted from our very souls if we could take hold of forgiveness like Christ forgives. He accepted all that we would ever do wrong at the cross and paid the price for it unconditionally. He did not say, "If they cross this line, I'm getting down from this cross and

I'm going on about my business." No, He decided that obedience to His Father's will was a better plan than not sacrificing of his own body. He stayed on the cross despite anything we would do, even today!

In Luke 9:23-24, Jesus tells us that if we desire to be like Him, we must first deny ourselves, then take up our cross daily and follow Him. Decide today that walking like Christ in forgiveness of what your spouse does today is more important than holding on to his sins. No, you are not a doormat, and no, you should not allow your spouse to abuse you in any kind of way. If you feel threatened in any way, by anyone, please get to a place of safety. But, beyond that, don't allow what your husband does today to stop you from being more like Christ. Be committed to becoming a change agent for forgiveness today. Once you let go and let God, others will see His work in you and follow suit. God's word never comes back void! (Isaiah 55:11)

"WHAT TO DO" IF YOU FAIL: Do something radical today. If your spouse does something to offend you, do the opposite of what you wanted to do. If you wanted to slap him, hug him instead. If your first thought was to give him a few choice words, instead shower him with the very opposite. Yes, this is hard, but so is living in an unfruitful marriage. Try it! You might like it! I know your spouse will. Kill him with kindness! Sometimes you must fake it until you make it. Your responses will become more natural in time.

💜 **HEART QUESTION:** Who or what in my past has stopped me from being able to forgive instantly? Why have I allowed this to linger in my life for so long?

_____

_____

_____

_____

_____

REFLECTION: List below the ways in which unforgiveness is affecting your physical health. Do you need to seek guidance from a counselor or spiritual mentor because of unforgiveness?

_____

_____

_____

_____

_____

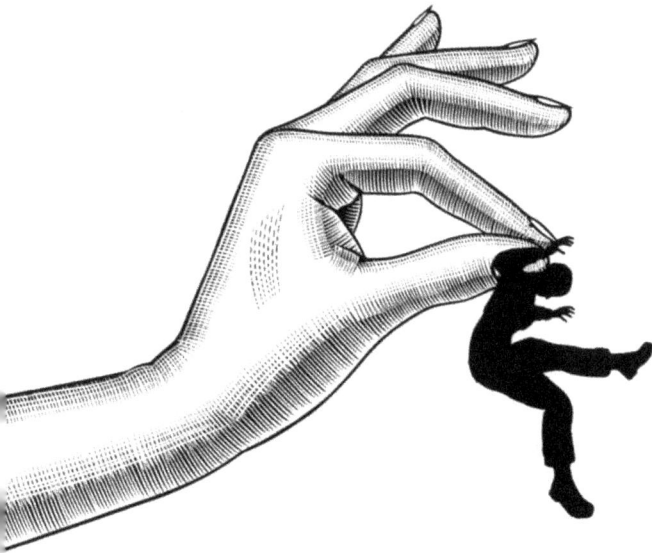

FORGIVENESS (DAY 5)

/fər giv'nis/ *The act of granting free pardon or remission for an offense*

DAILY AFFIRMATION: "I will walk in forgiveness of my husband's future offenses today."

MEMORY VERSE: *"Then Peter came to Jesus and asked, 'Lord, how many times shall I forgive my brother when he sins against me? Up to seven times?' Jesus answered, 'I tell you, not seven times but seventy-seven times.'"* **Matthew 18:21-22** NIV

HELPFUL HINTS: Isn't it awesome that God sees us in our completed form? He sees what we will be and not who we are right now. God can pardon our current faults and sins and look at us as finished products. Wouldn't it be awesome to follow suit and see our spouses as God sees them? Wouldn't it be wonderful not to expect our spouses to sin against us today? What a peaceful way to live. What if we believed that when our husbands wake today, they truly don't have an intention in the world to harm us?

Well, the reality is, that is how God sees us. He is constantly in our corner, expecting us to do right by Him. He and the enemy are at opposite ends of our courts, waiting to see whose team we are going to play on today. Will it be God and His angels or the enemy and his demons (Hebrews 12:1)?

In our scripture today, we find Peter in the very same predicament regarding forgiveness. Like Peter, when it comes to our spouses, we want to know when enough is enough. According to Jesus, forever is never enough. It is important, though, to remember that forgiveness and the ability to set boundaries in relationships are two very different things. You can forgive without allowing habitual behaviors to continue to damage your marriage and family. Boundaries are a healthy part of any great relationship, but even boundaries begin with forgiveness. Let's deliberately try to walk in a constant state of forgiveness of our husbands, starting today. Change begins with us.

"WHAT TO DO" IF YOU FAIL: Give him the benefit of the doubt today, even when you can't see how anything he is doing or saying will benefit you. Expect the expected today. Lift the demands off your husband. For example, if your husband is chronically late, expect him to be late and make the best of a bad situation. Overdo what you would normally do in order to make up for his shortcomings. Let today be a day when you give of yourself 120% without expecting a return. Don't keep the receipt on your giving today; you don't want to return or exchange it.

HEART QUESTION: Why is it easier for me to hold a grudge than to forgive?

_____

_____

_____

_____

_____

_____

REFLECTION: What is my true definition of grace and mercy? Can I truly live up to what I expect others to give to me regarding grace and mercy?

_____

_____

_____

_____

_____

_____

_____

_____

_____

_____

_____

_____

_____

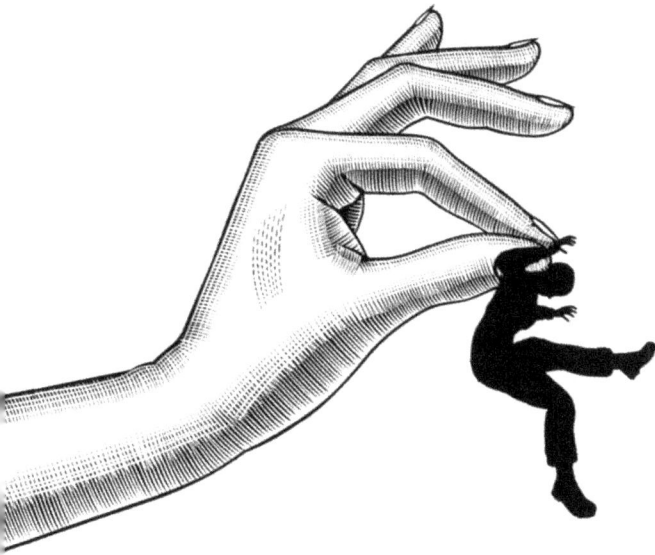

FORGIVENESS (DAY 6)

/fər giv'nis/ *The act of granting free pardon or remission for an offense*

DAILY AFFIRMATION: "I will embrace forgiveness in every area of my life as a wife today."

MEMORY VERSE: *"Bear with each other and forgive whatever grievances you may have against one another. Forgive as the Lord forgave you."* **Colossians 3:13** NIV

HELPFUL HINTS: By now, you ought to be a walking, talking pillar of forgiveness. Our primary desire as believers should be to walk in forgiveness in every area of our lives. If forgiveness is not one of our primary goals, then we truly need to evaluate if we are who we say we are. Freedom and peace are a

byproduct of forgiveness. Dr. Guy Pettit states that "the forgiveness process is simply the cancelation of all the conditions in the mind that are blocking the flow of love and life energy, independently of the behavior of others." When we don't forgive, we literally take time off our lives. Life is too short to deliberately take your own time into your own hands. Make the choice today to choose to add to your life, rather than taking away from it.

Forgiveness should be a mandatory way of life for you now. You should be able to see its benefits manifesting in your life. Hold on to the peace that forgiveness brings. Even now, the enemy will be on the hunt, waiting for an opportunity to see if you will forgive or not. But remember, your life truly depends on it. There aren't too many things we go through in life for ourselves. We are vessels fit for God's use today. We can forgive as the Lord forgives us!

"WHAT TO DO" IF YOU FAIL: Remember when we were in school (I might be dating myself!), and we would have to write lines for punishment? "I will not talk out of turn in class," or "I will not throw food in the cafeteria." Well, when you fail today, write today's affirmation and scripture as many times as you are able. The whole premise behind writing lines was to remind us not to go down the same road again. Hand cramps helped us then, and they will do the same for us now. Remember, this is a life-or-death situation.

💜 **HEART QUESTION:** How do you feel right before you are about to give up on something?

_____

_____

_____

_____

_____

_____

REFLECTION: What steps can you take before you have that "I'm about to give up" feeling to prevent that behavior? List them below and make them a part of your life routine.

_____

_____

_____

_____

_____

_____

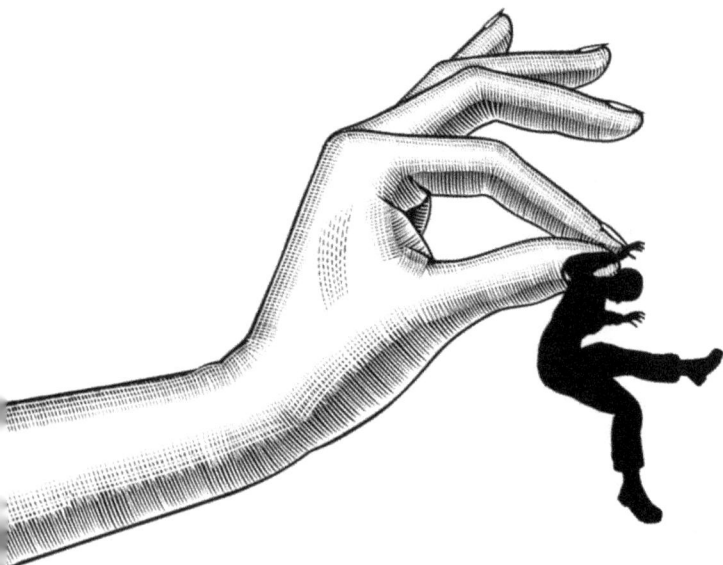

FORGIVENESS (DAY 7)

/fər giv'nis/ *The act of granting free pardon or remission for an offense*

DAILY AFFIRMATION: "I will forgive like Christ forgives, all day in all things."

MEMORY VERSE: *"But love ye your enemies, and do good, and lend, hoping for nothing again; and your reward shall be great, and ye shall be the children of the Highest: for he is kind unto the unthankful and to the evil."* **Luke 6:35** KJV

HELPFUL HINTS: Forgiveness is seeping out of your pores, right? In thinking about the journey of forgiveness, I am reminded of the 2006 movie *Click* starring Adam Sandler as Michael Newman, who gets an opportunity to fast-forward through many rough parts of his life

with an altruistic universal television remote. The character ends up fast-forwarding through many arguments with his wife, traffic jams, and difficulties at work in hopes of making his life easier. Unfortunately, he ends up fast-forwarding through large but good parts of his life and reaches a dismal end.

Aren't we just like that when it comes to forgiveness? We want to walk in the spirit of forgiveness without the lessons we learn from going through the hurt and pain that lead us to it. Our scripture is very clear about commanding us to love constantly and consistently. This adage always includes forgiveness. Our steps to forgiveness should be very clear by now: 1. Forgiveness is mandatory in the life of a believer. 2. We must make a conscious choice to do it. 3. Forgiveness is a process that must be practiced consistently. 4. Forgiveness is more beneficial to the giver than to the receiver. 5. There are boundaries that should be set up in relationships, but forgiveness is endless. 6. We are being most like Christ when we forgive. Surely our husbands will benefit from a woman who is walking consistently down a path of forgiveness. Embrace your new "forgiveness" lifestyle today.

"WHAT TO DO" IF YOU FAIL: You have several strategies now when it comes to getting back up on the forgiveness horse. Review what has worked best for you in the last six days and use that plan in the event you fall off. Remember, this is not a

one-day journey, it is a life process. Ask the Holy Spirit to help you keep your best forgiveness plans in mind. Remember that forgiveness is giving up the hope that the past will change. If you plan to remain married, then you do this as many times as you need to.

💟 **HEART QUESTION:** How do you think your life would be if you could fast-forward through all the rough stuff? Would that be helpful or harmful?

_____

_____

_____

_____

_____

_____

_____

_____

_____

_____

_____

REFLECTION: Use the space below to write down the hardest lesson you've learned from having to forgive your husband when you didn't want to. Discuss here if you feel like you have overcome your inability to forgive.

_____

_____

_____

_____

_____

_____

_____

_____

_____

_____

_____

_____

_____

_____

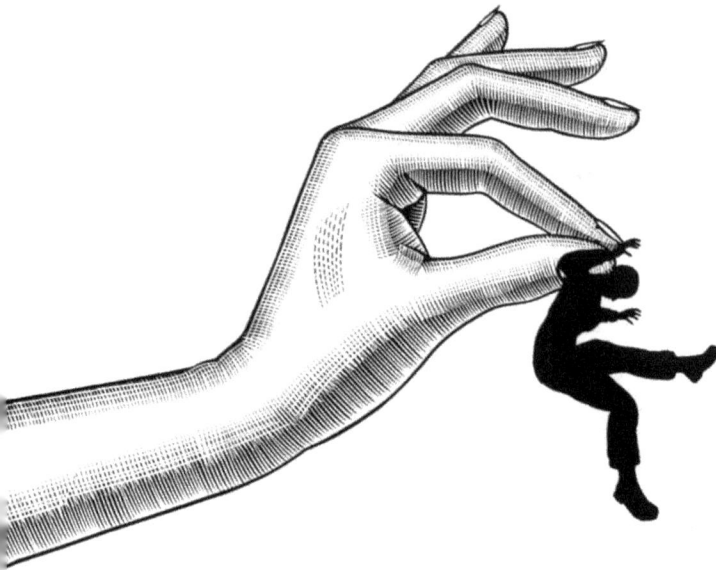

OBEDIENCE (DAY 8)

/ō bē'dē ə̄ns/ *The state of complying or following commands or restrictions of one in authority*

DAILY AFFIRMATION: "I will walk in obedience to the will of my Father in all things today."

MEMORY VERSE: *"And ye shall be holy unto me: for I the Lord am holy, and have severed you from other people, that ye should be mine."* **Leviticus 20:26** KJV

HELPFUL HINTS: In this passage of scripture, God is speaking to His people Israel. He laid down the laws regarding impurity and unholy living, and He expected them to abide by those laws. He was so serious about His command for them to be obedient that He also issued out specific punishments for the sins committed, which almost always included death (read

Leviticus chapter 20). Because born-again believers have been saved by grace and by the blood of the Lamb, they often slip by committing some of these same sins without immediate ramifications. But God is as serious now as He was when He formulated the laws for the Israelites. No, immediate death may not come, but judgment for sins is inevitable.

God is calling us to a place of holiness. In a sense, He has sectioned us off from the world so that we can be His Top Models. *America's Next Top Model* was a very popular show in the early 2000s that I watched all the time. One of the most consistent things about the show was that, week after week, the judges were looking for a steady increase or improvement in the girls' skills as aspiring models. Don't you think our God who is the highest judge has somewhat of the same standards?

Choose today that living a life of obedience is better than any temporary thrill. God is jealous, and He has already told you He wants you to be His completely. Remember, though, God's girls are holy and obedient. His wives are set apart for good works. Aren't you tired of being on the wrong team?

"WHAT TO DO" IF YOU FAIL: If we are honest, we all fall prey to disobedience at times. Disobedience always brings on consequences. Think of the worst thing that could happen to your marriage right now. Write it down and slip it in your pocket. Now imagine it happening every time you feel yourself wanting to take the easy road of disobedience today. Check your pocket periodically to remind yourself of what you could be heading toward in your marriage. Remember, you can choose your sin, but you cannot choose the consequences.

HEART QUESTION: List one thing that you know God has called you to be obedient to as a wife, but you have been refusing to do.

_____

_____

_____

_____

_____

_____

_____

REFLECTION: Now that you have refreshed your memory about your disobedience, write down below what you think might happen if you decided, just for one day, to do what God told you to do. Ponder the blessings you have been missing because of disobedience. Make a conscious choice to obey in that area, and set your intentions to do it. It may be difficult, but what worth having comes easy?

_____

_____

_____

_____

_____

_____

_____

_____

_____

_____

_____

_____

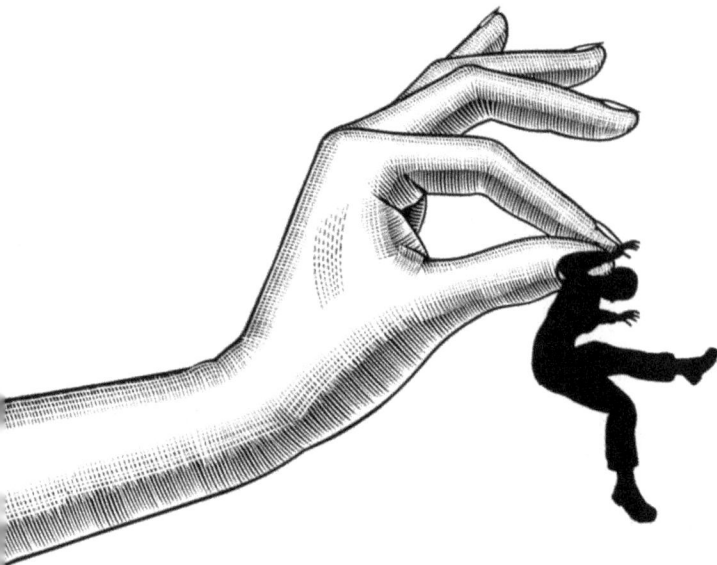

OBEDIENCE (DAY 9)

/ō bē'dē ᴓns/ *The state of complying or following commands or restrictions of one in authority*

DAILY AFFIRMATION: "I choose to walk in obedience to my Father's will regarding my duties as a wife today."

MEMORY VERSE: *"Don't you know that when you offer yourselves to someone to obey him as slaves, you are slaves to the one whom you obey—whether you are slaves to sin, which leads to death, or to obedience, which leads to righteousness?"* **Romans 6:16** NIV

HELPFUL HINTS: You have two choices to make today: you can either do it God's way or not. His way leads to life and peace, and the opposite leads to instant gratification but inevitably death and decay in your marriage. Choose obedience at all costs today. It is a simple choice. Think beyond your circumstances today. What if God would allow you, like Ebenezer Scrooge in *A Christmas Carol*, to see how your marriage plays out because of your disobedience? What would that picture look like? Too many times, we let our intuition and feminine instincts overrule our common sense. If God said it, then we should do it! Don't waste your time today focusing on your way. Mediate on 2 Corinthians 10:13. God will provide a way out. God is faithful and will honor your obedience.

"WHAT TO DO" IF YOU FAIL: It makes no sense to wallow in disobedience. We have already learned how to forgive ourselves, so begin there today when and if you fail in this area. Secondly, do something simple: reward yourself for the good that you do today. Nothing expensive or extravagant, but maybe pay yourself a compliment if you are able to hold your tongue when you don't want to. Allow yourself a few minutes of quiet time. Dance to your favorite song. Your mind and body will begin to like what you do for it when it behaves. It will be difficult to disobey when you reward yourself for obedience. Best practices in Early Childhood education call this "positive rewards for good behavior."

💜 **HEART QUESTION:** What is the main thing that prevents you from wanting to obey God's word regarding being a wife?

_____

_____

_____

_____

_____

REFLECTION: If you had a dollar for every time you disobeyed God in your marriage, would you be a rich woman or a pauper right now? Reflect below on how that makes you feel.

_____

_____

_____

_____

_____

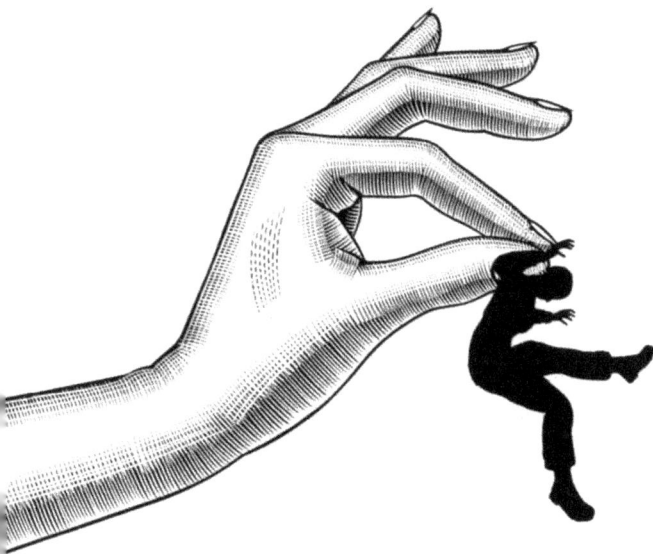

OBEDIENCE (DAY 10)

/ō bē'dē ₔns/ The state of complying or following commands or restrictions of one in authority

DAILY AFFIRMATION: "I will walk in obedience expressed through love toward my husband today."

MEMORY VERSE: *"And the second is like it: 'Love your neighbor as yourself.'"* **Matthew 22:39** NIV

HELPFUL HINTS: What closer neighbor do you have than the one who lives with you? Sometimes because of our circumstances, it is easier to love someone we don't know versus the one who seems to know how to push the wrong buttons in us so well. Reflect today on the benefits of being angry at your spouse. We can say that we love our husbands unconditionally, but

when they make us mad, unfortunately a little bit of that love goes flying out of the window! But is it worth it? Are those moments of anger beneficial? Are we walking in righteous anger like Christ did when he beat the moneychangers out of the temple, or are we walking in our own self-righteousness (Mark 11:15-17)?

We must be so very careful that our anger toward our husbands, even in small things, does not mount up in our hearts. If you continue to sweep small piles of dirt under a rug, eventually it makes a huge heap. Unresolved anger leads to bitterness and our old friend unforgiveness. Do yourself a favor and don't go down that road. Pray today that you understand how your husband receives love best. Does he like affirming words, affection or quality time? Is he appreciative of acts of service, or does he like gifts? Once you study and learn his love language, express love toward him in that way today, continually and constantly. Check out Dr. Gary Chapman's book on love languages if you need more clarity here.

"WHAT TO DO" IF YOU FAIL: Loving obediently can be a tough thing. It pulls you out of your comfort zone and pushes you to do things you would prefer not to do. When you find yourself walking in something other than love for your husband today, write him a little note or text expressing your love toward him. Yes, this will be uncomfortable and unnatural,

especially when you are mad, but do it anyway! There will be no change unless you change!

💜 **HEART QUESTION:** In what ways do you command obedience in your roles of authority, say, with your children or people who work for you? Why is this important to you?

_____

_____

_____

_____

_____

REFLECTION: Discuss here why you fell in love with your husband. Write down 20 reasons why you believed you loved him when you got married. Are those reasons still valid, or have they changed completely?

_____

_____

_____

_____

_____

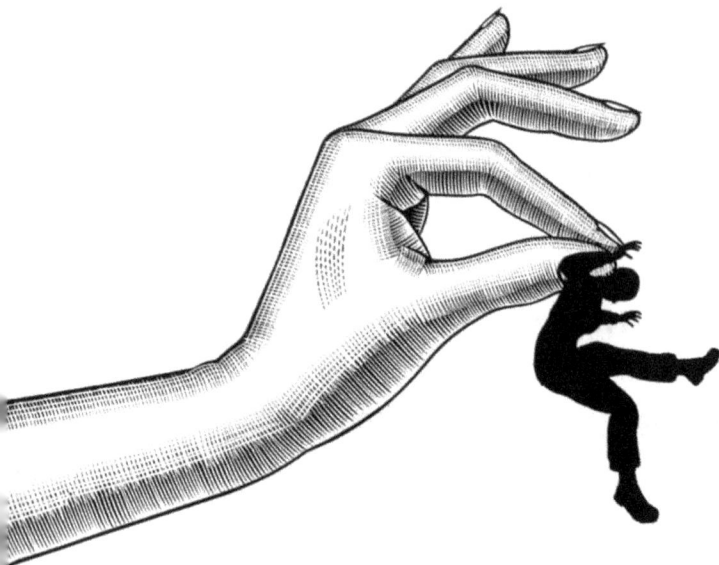

OBEDIENCE (DAY 11)

/ō bē'dē ᵊns/ *The state of complying or following commands or restrictions of one in authority*

DAILY AFFIRMATION: "I will walk in obedient respect for my husband today."

MEMORY VERSE: *"Set a guard over my mouth, O Lord; keep watch over the door of my lips."* **Psalm 141:3** NIV

HELPFUL HINTS: Interesting scripture to match today's affirmation, huh? Yes, our respect or lack thereof begins in our minds, but it is spewed through our mouths. We can kill a brother faster with our lips than a assault rifle can catch him in the heart. No, we don't need physical weapons. We have learned to craft our mouths instead. Some might say a woman's

tongue is sharper than any two-edged sword. It can cut a husband's confidence going in and coming out!

Often, we insist on using our tongues as weapons because of our vulnerability as women. We are typically looked at as the weaker vessel, so we use one of the strongest muscles in the human body to overcompensate for it. Many of our tongues have overuse injuries, especially when it comes to our husbands! If we are not talking to him about something negative, we are talking to someone about him negatively.

Don't play yourself today. Life and death are in the power of the tongue (Proverbs 18:21). If you could see all the death you are causing in your husband with your little bitty words, you might rethink your next statement to him. It might be your last; you just might kill him! To guard means to protect from harm. Ask God to be that guard over your mouth today. He will do it; He is faithful.

"WHAT TO DO" IF YOU FAIL: Put yourself on a talk fast today when you feel yourself falling. Decide not to say a word for 10 minutes or an hour if you can. During that time, reflect on how to use choice words, ones that edify and don't tear down. Jot down some things you learn about yourself when you make yourself shut up for a moment. You don't always have to have the last word.

💜 **HEART QUESTION:** Has the last word always been yours in an argument? If so, why? How does that type of winning make you feel?

_____

_____

_____

_____

_____

REFLECTION: What is the main thing you keep nagging your husband about that he has done nothing to fix or change, regardless of your rants and raves? What might be a better approach regarding this situation, and how will you go about achieving it?

_____

_____

_____

_____

_____

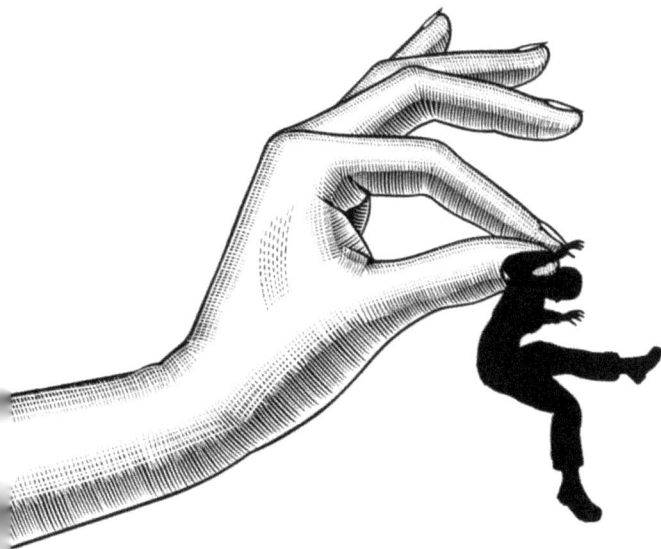

OBEDIENCE (DAY 12)

/ō bē'dē ∂ns/ *The state of complying or following commands or restrictions of one in authority*

> **DAILY AFFIRMATION:** "I will obediently encourage my husband to walk in his destiny today."

> **MEMORY VERSE:** *"A father can give his sons homes and riches, but only the Lord can give them understanding wives."* **Proverbs 19:14** TLB

HELPFUL HINTS: Obedience is a gift that is like a faucet. Once you turn it on, it can replenish and water anything and everything that is in its path. When you decide to be obedient as a wife, you cannot direct the flow, but you can manage the stream. Today, shift your focus on to how you can impact

your husband's purpose through your own obedience. Are you being a good example to him and those around him by finishing what you started? Is your purpose in life known to others, and can they see real-time evidence that you are fulfilling that purpose?

Modeling is the best example and can be powerful encouragement. You husband's purpose might be lying dormant because of where yours is lying. Be intentional about the plans for your life, whether your purpose is to start a business, go back to school, or get into better shape. We want to be intentional about following God's plans for our lives, and surely those around you who notice will eventually begin to attack their own purpose. Take your focus off your husband's walk and focus on yours. Even though he is the head, when you line up, he will eventually line up. Sow good seeds today into your own purpose, and encourage your husband gently by your actions to fulfill his. God has great things for the both of you. It will work in God's timing, not yours.

"WHAT TO DO" IF YOU FALL OFF: Today when you want to nag or harass your husband about his purpose, instead do something that lines up with your own purpose. Refocus that energy into something for yourself. Finish your own budget; start the outline for the book you are going to write. Check up on your office space for your business. Do something for yourself and let God do something for your spouse.

💜 **HEART QUESTION:** List one way that your obedience might influence your husband in fulfilling his purpose.

_____

_____

_____

_____

_____

REFLECTION: In the space below, write down some ways that you can "passively" help your husband fulfill his destiny. These should be things that you know could impact him, but not force him into moving into alignment with his goals. Ask God to give you a revelation regarding how to execute and implement these strategies in your daily life.

_____

_____

_____

_____

_____

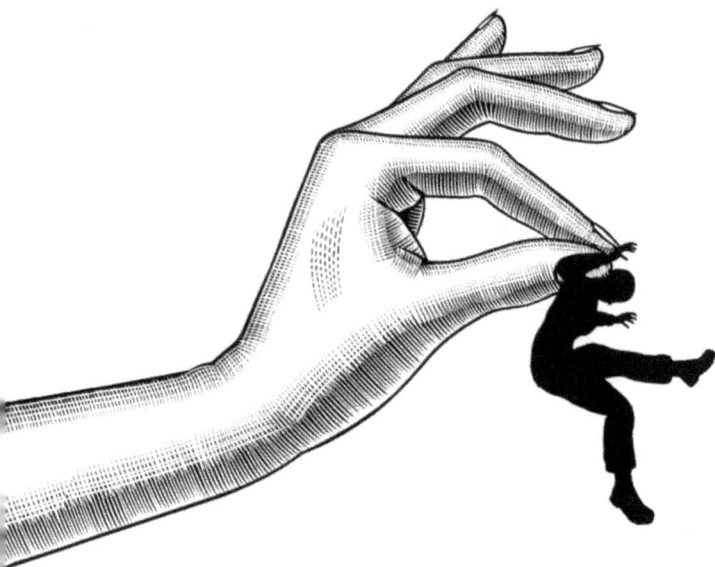

OBEDIENCE (DAY 13)

/ō bē′dē ∂ns/ *The state of complying or following commands or restrictions of one in authority*

DAILY AFFIRMATION: "I will walk in obedience regarding my mouth toward my husband today."

MEMORY VERSE: *"The tongue that brings healing is a tree of life, but a deceitful tongue crushes the spirit."* **Proverbs 15:4** NIV

HELPFUL HINTS: Wow, what a tough pill to swallow. We let our mouths get us in trouble constantly. My problem is sarcasm. I have let it get in the way of my family having peace just because I chose it over keeping my mouth closed. Proverbs 10:19 (TLB) says, *"Don't talk so much. You keep putting your foot in your mouth. Be sensible and turn off the flow!"* It

can be so challenging to decide not to use the biggest weapon we have against our husbands and just be quiet. We decide that being "Holy Ghost junior" will fix our husbands or the crisis at hand instead. Typically, it only makes it worse. The only thing that will work against our "mouth-weapon" is the real Holy Spirit.

Decide today that your mouth will not win over righteousness. You must first give your mouth over to the Lord in prayer and make it subject unto Christ in all your conversations. Secondly, you should use your accountability partner to hold you to whatever you say you are going to do regarding taming your tongue. Lastly, you must set a penalty for going against your plan. We kill seconds off our marriages every time we use our mouths in spite. It can be depressing to think about controlling your mouth, because if you are like me, we just like to talk, and honestly, most of the time it's pretty good stuff! But is talking more important than preventing a divorce because you wouldn't shut it up? Is your mouth worth your children growing up with their parents in separate homes? I dare think not. What do you have to lose? Today is the day. Give up the spite, the sarcasm, the hatefulness, and the revenge that pours out of your mouth, and choose His way.

"WHAT TO DO" IF YOU FALL OFF: Determine what your consequences will be for using your tongue as a weapon against your husband today. Maybe you give up that afternoon snack. Maybe you fast from talking for one hour. Maybe you give up watching your favorite TV program, or better yet, maybe you make yourself go exercise and work some other parts of your body. Whatever it is, decide to try to implement the consequence every time you fall off. Soon, you will desire to serve Christ with your mouth more than sacrificing your favorite things.

HEART QUESTION: Write down the last time you embarrassed your husband by using your mouth inappropriately. How did you determine that you embarrassed him?

_____

_____

_____

_____

_____

_____

REFLECTION: Begin in the space below to generate your thoughts about writing a letter to your husband about the incident above. Include an apology in the letter, and discuss how you plan to prevent that episode from happening again. Pray over the letter, place it on his pillow or mail it to him, and wait for God to work.

_____

_____

_____

_____

_____

_____

_____

_____

_____

_____

_____

_____

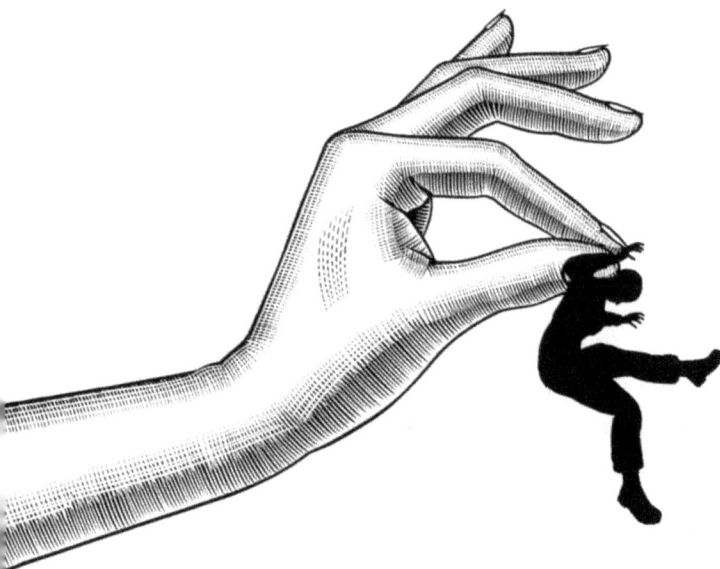

OBEDIENCE (DAY 14)

/ō bē'dē ∂ns/ *The state of complying or following commands or restrictions of one in authority*

DAILY AFFIRMATION: "I set myself in position to be obedient to God's will as a wife today."

MEMORY VERSE: *"Remind the people to be subject to rulers and authorities, to be obedient, to be ready to do whatever is good."* **Titus 3:1** NIV

HELPFUL HINTS: Be ready to be obedient today! You will have multiple opportunities to serve Christ in your obedience. The enemy is ready to make you rebel, but you must cast him off. You have the power to do so. You realize now that your obedience in marriage is a must and not a privilege. If you stay in order regarding obedience, your whole family lines up.

It is impossible for your husband and children to remain out of order when you line up, simply because God is not the author of confusion. It may not be a quick fix, but change will occur. It may not change the way you want it to, but change will occur.

He desires for all things to be done decently and in order (1 Corinthians 14:40). I guarantee that when you do your part, God will do His. Forget about what your husband is not doing. Endure hardness as a good soldier of Jesus Christ (2 Timothy 2:3). Don't worry your pretty little self about it, just obey God today. He will take care of the rest. Your obedience will be like yeast in bread: a little makes the whole loaf rise. Watch the bread of your marriage rise to the occasion because you decided to do what God tells you. He is not a man that he should lie, nor change His mind, when He speaks, He acts and what He promises He fulfills (Numbers 23:19). Praise God right now for the victory!

"WHAT TO DO" IF YOU FALL OFF: When you are disobedient today, guess what: start over. You will have another opportunity before you know it to allow good to prevail over evil. The life of a believer is a work in progress. We should only question it when we refuse to move forward and constantly go back to our old ways. If you are constantly choosing self over God's way, this may be a moment to check your belief system. Believe God and then work on your obedience. It is as simple as that. "It's deep but it's not that deep," as one of my sisters likes to say.

💜 **HEART QUESTION:** How do you feel when your children or subordinates at work are compliant with your plan? God feels the same way. Don't you want Him to feel that way today? Write down your thoughts about compliance here.

_____

_____

_____

_____

_____

REFLECTION: List below the times in the past seven days when you have prevailed in obedience to God as a wife. Celebrate your victories with a praise party once you review your list. God is good, isn't He? He is faithful to His promises.

_____

_____

_____

_____

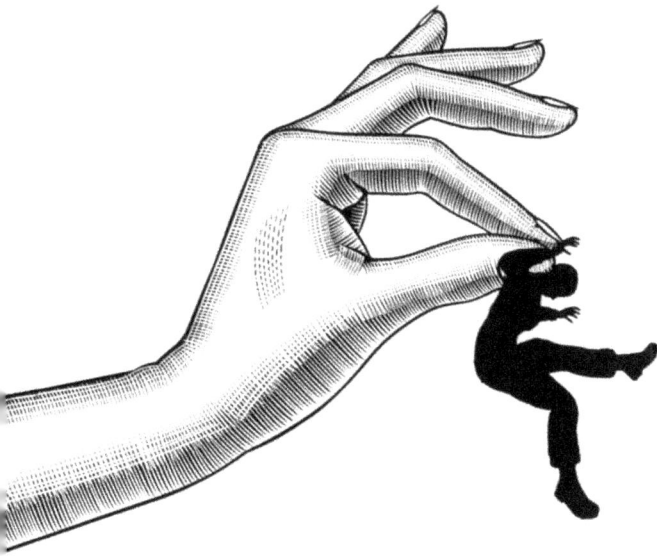

TRUST (DAY 15)

/trust/ The belief in and reliance on the integrity, strength, ability & surety of a person or thing

DAILY AFFIRMATION: "I trust God to care for me as a wife today."

MEMORY VERSE: *"Then He touched their eyes and said, 'According to your faith will it be done to you.'"* **Matthew 9:29** NIV

HELPFUL HINTS: Are you denying the favor of God in your marriage by refusing to trust Him to handle the changes that need to occur? Are you satisfied with managing your own mess? God is ready and well equipped with everything your marriage needs to survive. He often waits for us to give up the fight before He will step in. He wants the credit for our breakthroughs, and if He changes things in our lives while

we have our hands on it, we will surely decide that it was something that we did.

The challenge today is to let go enough to trust Him. This has nothing to do with your spouse today. Yes, your husband has made and will continue to make mistakes. He has done the same thing repeatedly, making you feel like there is no way you can trust again. But trusting God is a whole different ballgame. Trust for your marriage is based on God's greatness and not your spouse's abilities or inabilities.

Faith and trust go hand in hand. To trust God is to say, "I have enough faith to believe that He will supply all the needs of my marriage according to His riches and glory." Are you willing today? Are you willing to quit trusting yourself long enough to let God work? Today, you have entered the final stretch. You can do it! Trust God's timing today. Wait on Him and be of good courage. He can care for you as a wife right now. Lean on Him instead of your own understanding about your husband, and see if He does not show up in a big way.

"WHAT TO DO" IF YOU FALL OFF: When you forget to trust God, remind yourself at the next opportunity to wait double the time you waited previously. For example, if you responded in two minutes to something your spouse did not do, give yourself four minutes the next time. I believe God will honor your

patience. What's two more minutes of your life for God? He does not need much time; He just needs a willing heart.

💜 **HEART QUESTION:** List the last time you trusted God for something in your marriage and He came through like you thought He would. How do you feel about that situation now?

_____

_____

_____

_____

REFLECTION: In the space below, write one thing that you want to trust God for in your marriage, and then discuss with yourself and your accountability partner why you think it has not manifested yet. Ask your accountability partner to pray for you the whole week regarding that situation.

_____

_____

_____

_____

_____

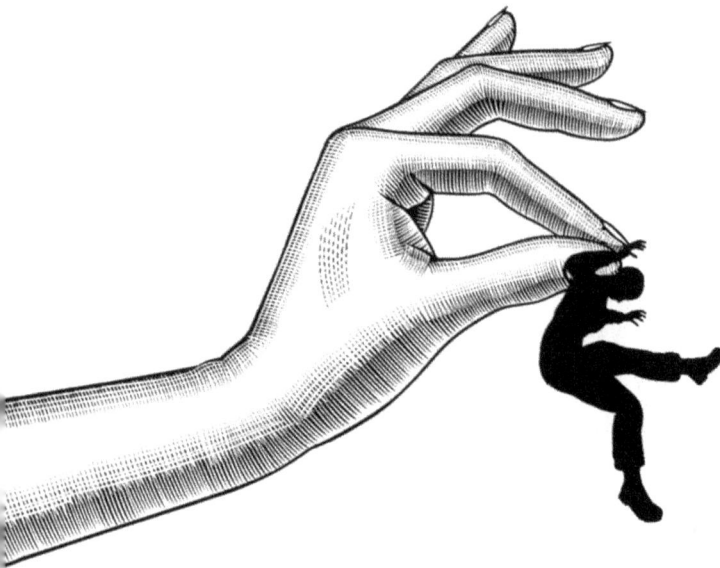

TRUST (DAY 16)

/trust/ The belief in and reliance on the integrity, strength, ability & surety of a person or thing

DAILY AFFIRMATION: "I deny my flesh the ability to doubt what God will do in me as a wife today."

MEMORY VERSE: "'Everything is possible for him who believes." Immediately the boy's father exclaimed, 'I do believe; help me overcome my unbelief!'" **Mark 9:23b-24** NIV

HELPFUL HINTS: It is so easy to look at your spouse or what he has done in the natural. You see his dirty underwear and socks on the floor, and you sigh. You see the cereal bowl he ate from yesterday on his computer desk with the milk ring in it, and you cringe. You have possibly even seen an unfamiliar

phone number in his pants pocket and felt a sense of panicked anger arise within you. All those things in the flesh could make any wife cringe.

And I am not suggesting that those things don't need to be addressed in some way, but it would be so much easier if we had the ability to see them with our spiritual eyes versus our natural ones. Flesh will turn on you in an instant. It will tell you that he will never change, that the number you found was his girlfriend's and that your marriage has ended. And in some instances, those things could be true, God forbid. But, if we could only look beyond what our natural eyes are telling us to what God sees, we could move forward in faith, sure that God was able to work above and beyond our flesh for our good.

Train your natural eyes to see differently. When you see what you see, instead look closer and focus in with the spiritual eyes God gave you to pierce through the natural. It's like looking through those kaleidoscopes when you were younger. The kaleidoscope signifies the fragments that come together to form a whole. Practically, you see only a part of the situation (the underwear on the floor), but it is not until you turn the scope that you see what was intended for you to see (your developing patience and deliverance from control and dominance). Turn your eyes inward to God's miracle for your marriage today. And know this one thing: *"For our light and momentary troubles are achieving for us an eternal glory that far outweighs them* all. So we fix our eyes not on what is seen, but on what is unseen. For what is seen is temporary, but what is unseen is eternal" (2 Corinthians 4:17-18.) NIV

"WHAT TO DO" IF YOU FALL OFF: When your flesh wants to jump off its rocker today, remember how much it costs every time you act in a negative way toward your husband. Change will begin with you. Ask the Holy Spirit to calm your spirit enough to see Him operating in all things. Grab that rubber band again from your previous forgiveness lessons and pop your flesh into believing that God is able. You must train your flesh into shape.

HEART QUESTION: Why do you choose the way of your flesh over God's way? What can you do to avoid that choice?

_____

_____

_____

_____

_____

_____

REFLECTION: Draw a stick figure of yourself in the space below and indicate where your spiritual "problem areas" are. Then problem-solve about how you can minimize these problems and turn them into solutions (read Matthew 5:30).

_____

_____

_____

_____

_____

_____

_____

_____

_____

_____

_____

_____

_____

_____

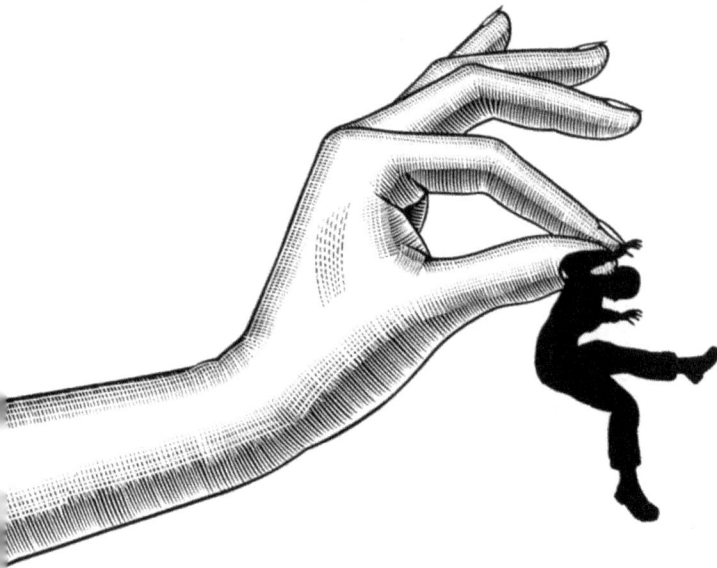

TRUST (DAY 17)

/trust/ The belief in and reliance on the integrity, strength, ability & surety of a person or thing

DAILY AFFIRMATION: "I will trust that the Holy Spirit has enough power to direct my husband today."

MEMORY VERSE: *"Do not let your hearts be troubled. Trust in God; trust also in me."* **John 14:1** NIV

HELPFUL HINTS: Sit down, Holy Ghost junior! You do not have to be the one your husband sings "Lead Me, Guide Me" to today. Firstly, despite what he has or has not done, he is a grown man capable of making decisions, whether they are good ones to you or not. None of us has a spotless track record when it comes to decision making. Chances are your husband did

not wake up this morning saying to himself, "What can I do today to make my wife upset?" If your husband is a believer for real, then I guarantee you he has the Holy Spirit available to him right now, just like you do if you believe. Even if he is not a believer, the Holy Spirit is able to work through and in any situation or circumstance.

Your constant prayer today must be, "Father, I trust you for my husband's life and for every decision he has to make today. You are able to lead and guide him along his way, and I believe that you will do what you are capable of." All day long, remember that God can lead and guide him better than you can. Listen, your leading has not been working anyway! Don't confuse letting go of trying to control him with not sharing wisdom with him when it is appropriate. Ask the Father to give you the right words to use when you feel led to share with him. Remember, you can catch more flies with honey than vinegar. Savor your words for your husband with the salt of the Holy Spirit and allow Him to direct his path.

"WHAT TO DO" IF YOU FALL OFF: Every time you get in the way of the Holy Spirit in your husband's life today, make note of it and, if possible, write that situation down or record it in a voice memo. At the end of the day, set aside 5-10 minutes to reflect on your mistakes. Spend some serious moments in prayer for repentance. Don't allow condemnation to set in

after this but rejoice that you are able to see your mistakes and be proactive about them.

💟 **HEART QUESTION:** Honestly ask yourself why you are trying to run your husband's life, or some parts of it. Read Genesis 3:16 in a version of the Bible that speaks to you. Are you acting like Eve or not?

_____

_____

_____

_____

_____

REFLECTION: Imagine your husband's life without you. How would it be different? Would it be better or worse? If you answered "better," what can you do to begin to turn your answer around?

_____

_____

_____

_____

_____

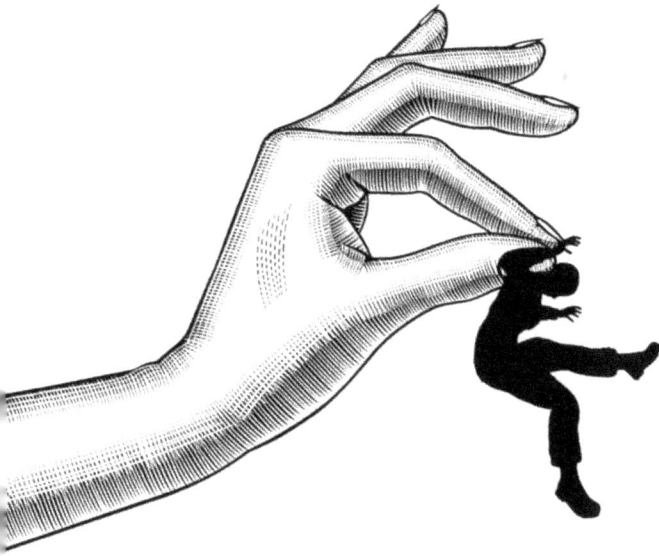

TRUST (DAY 18)

/trust/ The belief in and reliance on the integrity, strength, ability & surety of a person or thing

DAILY AFFIRMATION: "I will trust that my husband will honor his vows today."

MEMORY VERSE: *"For this cause shall a man leave his father and mother, and shall be joined unto his wife, and they two shall be one flesh."* **Ephesians 5:31** NIV

HELPFUL HINTS: Do you remember when your husband agreed to this: "I take you to be my wife, to have and to hold from this day forward, for better or for worse, for richer, for poorer, in sickness and in health, to love and to cherish; and I promise to be faithful to you until death parts us"? Just allow yourself to go back to that day for a moment. You were looking your

best, and your husband was fine as ever. He could have said anything to you at that moment and it would not have mattered, because you were in love!

Well, both of you made promises on that day that I am sure have been challenging to keep for one reason or another. Time can take the thrill and enthusiasm out of a relationship if you let it. But I believe today is a new day and that because of your prayers and faithfulness to change, your husband is now feeling the effects and wants to do something differently for you and your marriage. Allow him today to have you, to hold you through it all. Allow him to be faithful today. Don't push, pull, or begrudgingly force him to go against his vows; the promises he made before God and you. God is doing a miraculous work in you because you have given up your fight regarding your marriage and let Him handle it. Now the door is open for your husband to respond. Let him cherish his bride. It might be subtle, but it will happen.

"WHAT TO DO" IF YOU FALL OFF: You do not have to force this day on your husband. Allow God to work it out. Relax, this is your day. Without you having to say anything, your husband is going to show up in a fabulous way. Let him! It may not happen until the ninth hour, but God is going to honor your faithfulness. Look for his love even in the small things.

💜 **HEART QUESTION:** Have you changed since you got married, physically, spiritually, or emotionally? If yes, how?

_____

_____

_____

_____

_____

REFLECTION: Since you have reflected on how you used to be when you first got married, list below the things you wish you had not gotten away from. For example, maybe you kept yourself in better physical shape, maybe you had a better hairstyle, or maybe you prayed more frequently. Choose one of the things, and set a goal and a date to get back to how you were when he married you.

_____

_____

_____

_____

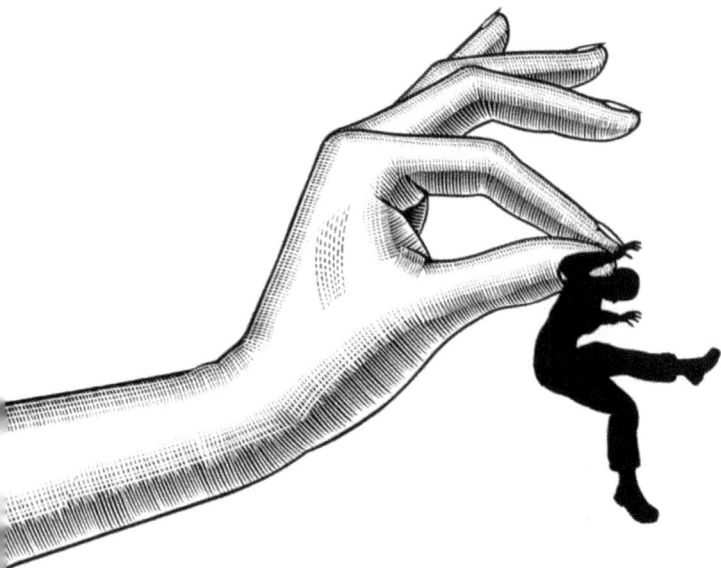

TRUST (DAY 19)

/trust/ The belief in and reliance on the integrity, strength, ability & surety of a person or thing

DAILY AFFIRMATION: "I will trust my ability to be the wife my husband needs today."

MEMORY VERSE: *"Ye are of God, little children, and have overcome them: because greater is he that is in you, than he that is in the world."* **1 John 4:4** NIV

HELPFUL HINTS: When John wrote this passage of scripture, he was speaking to new believers about testing the Spirits. He reminded them that there were many teachers and prophets who had gone out professing Christ but who really were not true believers. He cautioned them to use the Spirit inside of them to discriminate between those who had true faith

and those who had faith in the antichrist. Today, the same Holy Spirit equips us to be able to meet the needs of our husbands daily. We should no longer look to the world for answers as to how to be a wife. The world provides loopholes for wives when things don't go their way. The world says it's okay to take another lover or cuss your husband out when he wrongs you, or better yet, keep a mad money stash so that when he starts tripping, you will have a way out. We must literally turn ourselves away from the things of this world if we want the things of God.

Listen, ladies, it is a privilege to be a wife. Honor your privilege today by doing what you need to do to serve your husband. Trust your God-given abilities to meet his needs, especially when he doesn't deserve it. Yes, you may be tired, yes, you may be weary, but the Spirit never tires, and He will be the one doing the work if you allow Him to work through you. You are an overcomer in your marriage, and He lives inside you. He has set up camp in you and is able to conquer any obstacle that marriage puts in your path today.

"WHAT TO DO" IF YOU FALL OFF: Visualize yourself today as a wife who can meet the needs of her husband. Every need he has that does not cause you to sin should be your obligation today. When you see yourself going in the opposite direction, take 2-3 minutes to discuss the consequences with yourself. Even if you must excuse yourself from the situation, do so

to stay focused on your goal of trusting yourself to meet his needs today. By now, your husband has recognized your efforts. He wants to see you succeed, even if he does not show it.

💜 **HEART QUESTION:** Discuss here why trusting yourself has been a problem in the past.

_____

_____

_____

_____

_____

REFLECTION: Use the space below to develop an acronym for the word T R U S T. Memorize your acronym and use it as an affirmation all day, especially when you hit the rough spots and don't want to continue with your plans for today.

_____

_____

_____

_____

_____

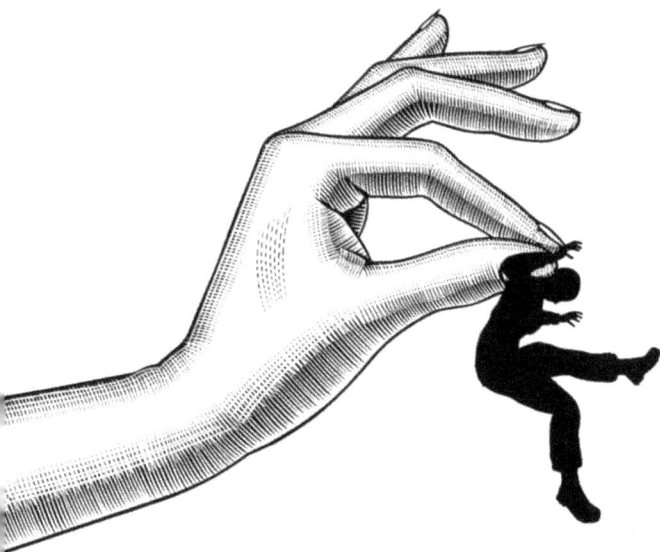

TRUST (DAY 20)

/trust/ *The belief in and reliance on the integrity, strength, ability & surety of a person or thing*

DAILY AFFIRMATION: "I trust God's word will safely guide me as a wife today."

MEMORY VERSE: *"So is my word that goes out from my mouth: It will not return to me empty, but will accomplish what I desire and achieve the purpose for which I sent it."* **Isaiah 55:11** NIV

HELPFUL HINTS: Let's be honest. Trusting God's word can be difficult sometimes, especially for us as wives. God continually challenges the core of wives by asking us to go against the very nature He created in us. He wants us to turn down the "multi-tasker" dial in our brain, relinquish the power we think we

have, and surrender our thoughts, opinions, and beliefs about our husbands over to Him so that He can do a new work in us. Have you ever gotten so busy doing so many things at once that you forget exactly what you are doing right in front of you? That is what happens when we neglect God's word. We hear His promises for us as wives but forget to stand on them. For example:

·   1 Corinthians 10:13 – When we are tempted, He will provide a way of escape.

·   2 Corinthians 5:17 – We are new creatures in Christ.

·   1 John 1:9 – He will forgive when we ask.

·   Titus 3:5 – He saves us because He loves us, not because of what we do.

So, we have these promises, but because we get busy doing us and everything else, we forget the simplicity of taking God at His word. Wives, we *must* commission our brains today to be like David and store up the word in our hearts so that we are committed to being sinless toward our husbands and ultimately toward God. His word needs to provide spiritual nourishment to our souls. Feast on His word today. Make it clear to your brain that the stinking thinking is over. Create new brain pathways today that are rooted in God's promises and His plan for your marriage and your life.

"WHAT TO DO" IF YOU FALL OFF: Reward yourself today when you forget God's word by taking 1-3 minutes to gather your thoughts and remember how good He is and that His grace is sufficient. Go to a quiet place (the john will do!). Reconnect with today's memory verse or a promise of God. Give your mind time to rest on that word. Refocus and get back to what you know is right. Do this several times today if needed. What's one minute of your life?

HEART QUESTION: Why is it easier to believe God's word and His promises for other people?

_____

_____

_____

_____

_____

_____

_____

_____

_____

_____

REFLECTION: Write about one time when you believed God's promises and it manifested in your life. How did that make you feel about God?

_____

_____

_____

_____

_____

_____

_____

_____

_____

_____

_____

_____

_____

_____

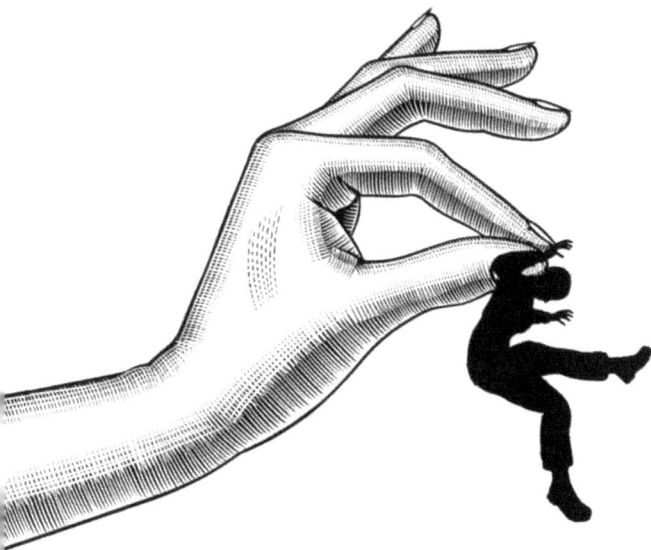

TRUST (DAY 21)

/trust/ The belief in and reliance on the integrity, strength, ability & surety of a person or thing

> **DAILY AFFIRMATION:** "I will trust in God completely today to bring forth His promises for me as a wife."

> **MEMORY VERSE:** *"There is surely a future hope for you, and your hope will not be cut off."* **Proverbs 23:18** NIV

HELPFUL HINTS: Some of God's promises are unconditional. For example, His Word states that He will never leave nor forsake us (Deuteronomy 31:6). In 2 Corinthians 12: 9-10, it is indicated that God's grace is sufficient for us. That's a promise only He can keep. We all need promises without conditions. But many of God's promises are conditional. John 3:16 tells us

that if any man believes in His Son, he shall reap the reward of eternal life. He first must believe, though. Several times in the biblical books of history, God told the Israelites that if they obeyed His laws, He would reward them with long life, fertility, and a prosperous land. We don't have to worry about God when it comes to promises. He is true to His word (Numbers 23:19).

So, what are the promises God has set aside for marriage? Well, let's check that out. In several web searches and reviewing biblical references on marriage, I did not find one single promise that God made for marriage except this one: Genesis 2:18, which says, *"The Lord God said, 'It is not good for the man to be alone. I will make a helper suitable for him.'"* All the other scriptures that deal with marriage are suggestions or commands for the husband and wife to partake in. Wow! How special we are as wives to be the subjects of His only direct promise toward marriage. The problem, then, is that we spend too much time trying to become this suitable helpmate instead of allowing God to make us one. Today, believe that you are special enough to God to make you over and over until you are completely suitable for your spouse.

"WHAT TO DO" IF YOU FALL OFF: Obtain an inexpensive amount of clay and mold it into a small object. You can use your kid's playdough if necessary. Make a flower, animal, or anything you like. When you slip up and forget who you are in Christ, mash your object up and make it over again. Now, depending on your day, this might become tedious. But the whole premise is that every time we mess up and fall off our marks, God is willing and able to make us over again! How awesome to be one of His children.

HEART QUESTION: List here what you think your spouse feels is a suitable helpmate. If you are feeling brave, pray first and then ask him what he thinks. See how what you thought matches up to his ideas.

_____

_____

_____

_____

_____

_____

_____

_____

REFLECTION: Use the space below to determine where God needs to make you over to fit your spouse's definition of "suitable."

_____

_____

_____

_____

_____

_____

_____

_____

_____

_____

_____

_____

_____

_____

_____

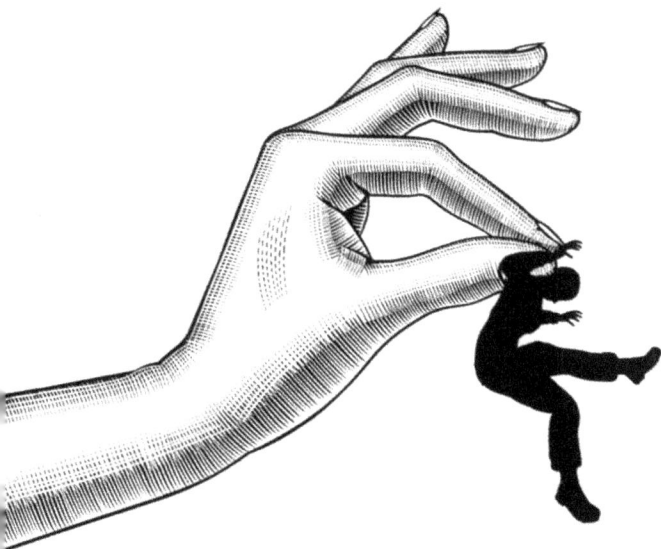

SUBMISSION (DAY 22)

/sǝb mish' en/ *The instance of giving over or yielding to the power or authority of another*

DAILY AFFIRMATION: "Submission is an assignment from God that I will submerse myself in today."

MEMORY VERSE: *"Wives, submit to your husbands as to the Lord."* **Ephesians 5:22** NIV

HELPFUL HINTS: Okay, I don't know about you, but most wives don't understand this word and run from it with swiftness. Willingly releasing your power and authority over to anyone can be difficult, but it becomes even more challenging when it is the person we are locked in covenant with. And God forbid he makes a mistake, like miss paying a bill on time or mishandle disciplining of the children. We can treat our

husbands like "one-hit wonders" when they mess up. We liked their song when it was popular, but as soon as it is off the top charts, we lose respect for them as artists.

Listen, in a Christian marriage, submission is not a choice, it is a command. If your marriage is in a chaotic state, check your submission meter. God will not allow a truly submissive wife to be overrun and abused. Be mindful of that passive-aggressive submission that allows your husband's sin to go unchecked. Submission is not equivalent to a being a doormat. If your husband is in a state of sin, you need to be in a state of prayer and move to a place of safety if his sin is mentally or physically damaging to you or your children. God didn't intend for any of His children to remain in a place of harm. Separate yourself from the immediate danger, and then seek healing or reconciliation only after intervention has taken place. Remember, you are lining up under God's plan and not your husband's plan.

"WHAT TO DO" IF YOU FALL OFF: Apply the "five-second rule" today when you feel yourself walking toward rebellion versus submission. Count to five in your mind… 1-2-3-4-5. Give yourself time to rethink the mistake and the sin you are about to fall into. Does the temporary satisfaction outweigh the blessings of God's plan? If so, move forward in your mess, but if it doesn't, and I know it doesn't, make a conscious decision to get back on your plan of doing it God's way.

💜 **HEART QUESTION:** Submission means to get up under a plan or a mission. Why can you do this so easily at work or in your church or civic organization?

_____

_____

_____

_____

_____

REFLECTION: Think about a specific time when you refused to submit to your husband. What were the results of your actions? Have they helped to forward or retard your marriage?

_____

_____

_____

_____

_____

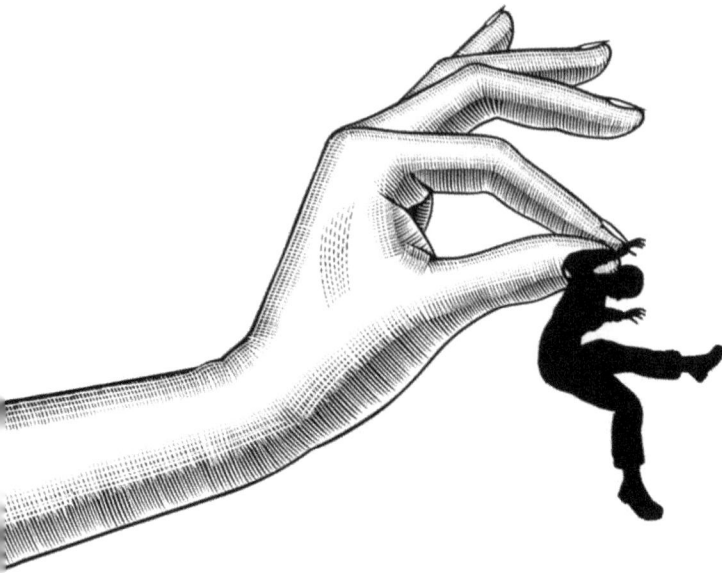

SUBMISSION (DAY 23)

/sǝb mish' en/ *The instance of giving over or yielding to the power or authority of another*

> **DAILY AFFIRMATION:** "There is safety in my ability to submit to God's will regarding my marriage today."

> **MEMORY VERSE:** *"Come to me, all you who are weary and burdened, and I will give you rest. Take my yoke upon you, and learn from me, for I am gentle and humble in heart, and you will find rest for your souls."* **Matthew 11:28-29** NIV

HELPFUL HINTS: God provides submission in marriage as a prize, not a punishment. You are God's precious daughter. He designed the gift of submission specifically to allow you to rest in, abide in, and find peace in the fact that your husband is in charge.

One of my favorite ways to vacation used to be going on a cruise. Ideally, for seven days I would be subject to relaxation, all the great food I wanted, and great activities on the ship like ice skating and variety shows. For me, traveling that way was the best. I would sit around all day in the sun, partaking in spa treatments and tourist excursions. Not one time on that cruise did I have to worry about what time I'd have to be at work, what reports needed to be done, or if I had the right ingredients to make dinner. Honestly, even though my life was in the hands of a captain I did not know, I found myself in a state of "relaxation euphoria!" The only true responsibility I had was to accept or yield to the superior force or authority of the captain, his ship, and his rules.

Of course, I hear you saying, "Yeah, but my marriage ain't no cruise or vacation!" I will be the first one in line to admit that marriage isn't the easiest task on my list. We have hard work to accomplish as wives, but what God wants us to grasp is the whole feeling of safety, the "relaxation euphoria," that He has designed for us. We spend so much time trying to be the captain, and in many instances the ship itself, that we miss the opportunity to rest in the fact that at the end of the day, if the family sinks, the ultimate responsibility is not on us. Our husbands must answer to God as to why the ship is not afloat. Let that sink in for a moment.... The only reason you would have to answer about the conditions of the boat is if you have caused a mutiny and taken over. Calm down! End the standoff and relinquish the power back over to the proper authorities. God commands everything to be done in decency and in order. If you truly can find safety in the concept God designed especially for you, won't He be responsible enough to provide that net of support for you as a wife?

"WHAT TO DO" IF YOU FALL OFF: Find a specific worship song that speaks about resting in God, or the safety found in God. Put that song on your playlist in your car and on your home audio system. Listen to that song for the rest of the week, especially when you find that "mutiny" rising in you. Ask God to be faithful to His promise of giving rest to the weary, and wait for Him to work.

💜 **HEART QUESTION:** What life experience do you think has caused you to resist submission?

_____

_____

_____

_____

_____

_____

REFLECTION: Discuss here how you envision your marriage being different once you completely submit to God's plan for you as a wife.

_____

_____

_____

_____

_____

_____

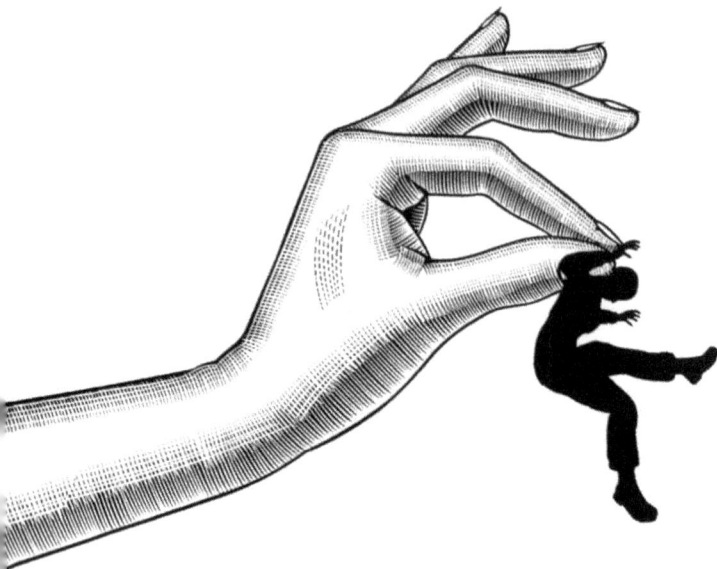

SUBMISSION (DAY 24)

/sǝb mish' en/ *The instance of giving over or yielding to the power or authority of another*

DAILY AFFIRMATION: "My ability to submit makes my husband's character shine."

MEMORY VERSE: *"Her husband is greatly respected when he deliberates with the city fathers."* **Proverbs 31:23.** MSG

HELPFUL HINTS: Let's just face it! Our men want the respect of other men – well, everybody, for that matter. They want to be noted as someone who has it all together, and there is no better way to show this off than by having a woman who has his back in all things. Their ego has plenty to do with this, but don't cut the brother up so fast for this. He was made in God's image, and we know that even though our Father

does not need our worship and praise, He does require it and desire it from us (John 4:23-24). Our husbands desire praise from us even when they don't deserve it, and you submitting to that fact and giving respect even when it is not necessarily warranted is exactly what God is looking for. And yes, men want praise for everything and often. You cannot compare your multitasking abilities to his single-task abilities. Yes, you give baths, comb hair, check homework, and cook dinner all in a single bound. Men are not wired that way, and to minimize his abilities because you don't think they match yours is egregious and sinful!

When your man hears from you, "Honey, for real, you are the best garbage man this house has! You always meet the truck on time, and you even put another bag in to replace the full one," this puffs his chest out, and even if he didn't do all of those things quite right, believe me, he is going to try his best to make it better next time. But to top that, let him hear you telling one of your girlfriends or co-workers about it. Baby, he will be breaking his neck to meet the garbage man next week! Men thrive on the opinion of their wives. They crave it, even though they don't ask for it. When his character is all polished up by you, he can function in his optimal state. Doesn't your car seem to drive better when it is washed, polished, and shined up? Even if it doesn't drive better, you drive it better because of the way it makes you feel. Submission is key in helping your husband drive his family better. He may not make all the right decisions, but if he still has someone who is in his corner, his cheerleader, even when he is losing, he will be equipped to seek God more diligently and seek wise counsel so he can make better choices. Don't you want to be a part of that?

"WHAT TO DO" IF YOU FALL OFF: Every time you speak poorly about your husband (to him directly or to someone else), YOU OWE HIM ONE! You can't take your words back, but you can apologize and replace those words of death with words of life. You owe him some words of affirmation for every time you have shamed or belittled him today.

HEART QUESTION: How do you think things would change in your household if you were to stop complaining about one thing your husband does wrong and start finding ways to make his character shine regarding that issue instead?

_____

_____

_____

_____

_____

_____

REFLECTION: Note how your husband responds when others compliment his character or something he does well. See how he responds, and discover ways you can evoke those same responses in him. Write them down and pray to make them a part of your daily regime.

_____

_____

_____

_____

_____

_____

_____

_____

_____

_____

_____

_____

_____

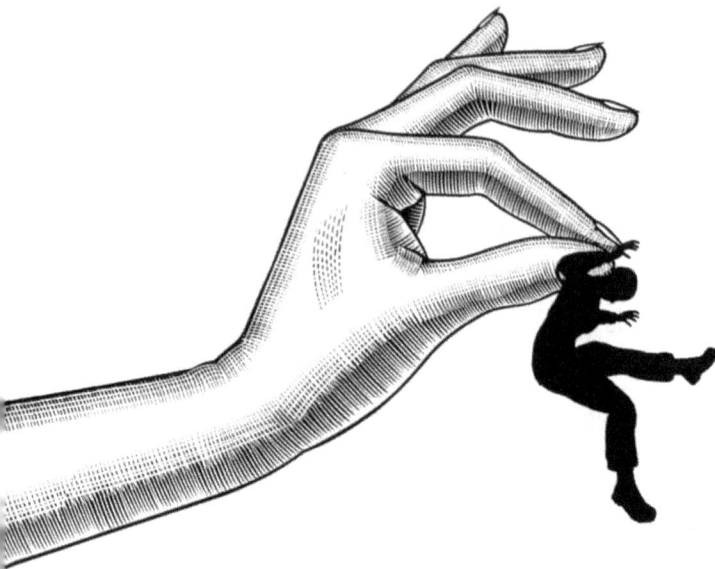

SUBMISSION (DAY 25)

/səb mish' en/ *The instance of giving over or yielding to the power or authority of another*

DAILY AFFIRMATION: "Because I am a submissive woman, my husband's job as protector is easier."

MEMORY VERSE: *"Obey your leaders and submit to them, for they are keeping watch over your souls, as those who will have to give an account. Let them do this with joy and not with groaning, for that would be of no advantage to you."* **Hebrews 13:17** ESV

HELPFUL HINTS: Our husbands have a job to do. And with some of us, that job is harder than others. Whether or not he knows or has accepted it, he is the *priest, provider, and protector* of his family and home. That doesn't mean he prays the longest, has the biggest income, or even has the biggest biceps! What it means is that the primary responsibility in those areas lies on him. He will be questioned about the spiritual growth of his family. If you do the budget and write the checks out in the family, he should be the one signing them, or at least he should know about them. And the physical strength thing, well, I will let that one fall where it may. However, if your husband is having difficulty fulfilling his duties in these areas, is it a fault of yours? Are you playing a role in his inability to perform because you are in the way? He may have come up short in the past, and he may need to prove worthy of these positions, but it is not your job to punish him until he meets some imaginary mark in your mind. Who died and made you judge?

Listen, submission is a figurative position. We don't have to physically bow down to our husbands' rule, but we willingly relinquish our ability to dominate and rule over the man that God placed over us. *NOTE: In no way am I supporting abuse in any form. If you have found yourself in an abusive situation, run and seek help today... Be safe.* However, if you, like me, are just one of those sisters who is independent and wants to "throw you' hands up at me," pipe down and see how much stress you take off your husband by letting him do his job alone. He can't watch over you with joy unless you let him. We want our children to do this, but are we willing to set the prime example in our homes by doing it ourselves?

"WHAT TO DO" IF YOU FALL OFF: Ask your husband to write down or discuss with you 2-3 things that make his job difficult as a husband. (Do not comment on them!) Today, when you get ready to flex your "unsubmissive" muscles, instead pray about one of those things and ask God to show you how you can make that easier for your husband.

HEART QUESTION: Why do I insist on crucifying my husband with my mouth in his greatest areas of weakness?

_____

_____

_____

_____

_____

_____

_____

REFLECTION: Do a quick internet study on King Henry VII of England. Discuss here why you think he was a successful king. Share how you think he was able to reach his success as king.

_____

_____

_____

_____

_____

_____

_____

_____

_____

_____

_____

_____

_____

_____

_____

_____

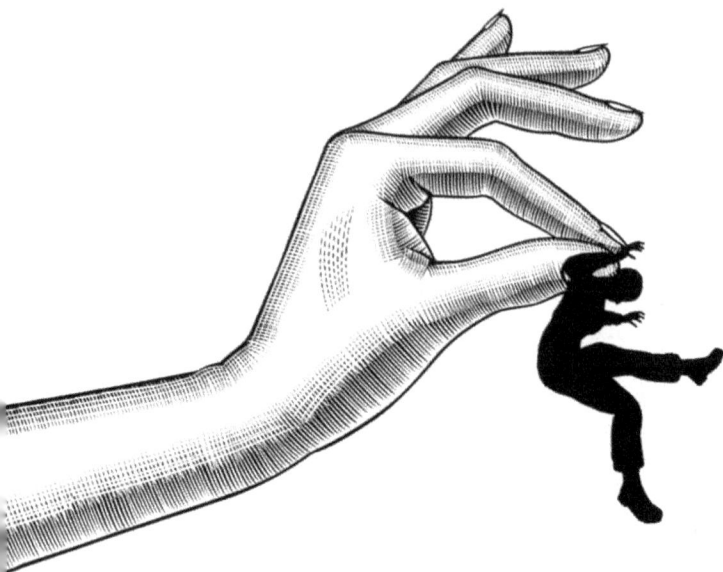

SUBMISSION (DAY 26)

/sǝb mish' en/ *The instance of giving over or yielding to the power or authority of another*

DAILY AFFIRMATION: "My reputation is enhanced because I am submissive to my husband."

MEMORY VERSE: *"In the same way, their wives are to be women worthy of respect, not malicious talkers but temperate and trustworthy in everything."* **1 Timothy 3:11** NIV

HELPFUL HINTS: Now, what does me gossiping have to do with my husband? Why do I have to watch what I say to my friends, and how in the world does that have anything to do with submission? As we have learned this week, submission is all about yielding your power. When we commit our mouths and our

language to the Lord, ultimately it makes our ability to submit in every area easier. Have you ever found yourself in a conversation with a girlfriend when she starts talking about her husband or someone else's husband in a negative way? She goes on and on about what he isn't doing right and what he did wrong. Before you know it, you are either agreeing with her or thinking about the last time your husband did the same thing. Next thing you know, you are off the phone and slamming your husband for something some other man did! Just admit it, we have all done it, but we don't have to keep doing it.

Our ability to keep watch over our mouths and what we say has a profound impact on how people view us and our husbands. Unfortunately, I have heard people tell my husband, "Man, you got a pistol for a wife, and I am praying for you, jack!" I used to think that was funny before I realized they were saying they were glad they were not him because of me. So basically, when I can submit to being a "gossipless," self-controlled, mild-mannered woman, I can expect the respect and honor that my marriage and husband deserve. Even though our husbands are in charge, there is a lot riding on us, huh?

"WHAT TO DO" IF YOU FALL OFF: Today, become an active listener. Practice listening to your co-workers or friends without participating in the drama. Commission your mouth to stand still. If you find this to be a problem, go to a quiet place for a

moment and remind your mouth who is in charge. Recondition your thinking and believe again that you can be a woman worthy of respect in all areas.

💗 **HEART QUESTION:** Why do my ears light up when I hear gossip?

_____

_____

_____

_____

_____

REFLECTION: Read James 3:2-12 today in your favorite translation of the Bible. Develop a short prayer about your "language weakness." Ask God for an intervention.

_____

_____

_____

_____

_____

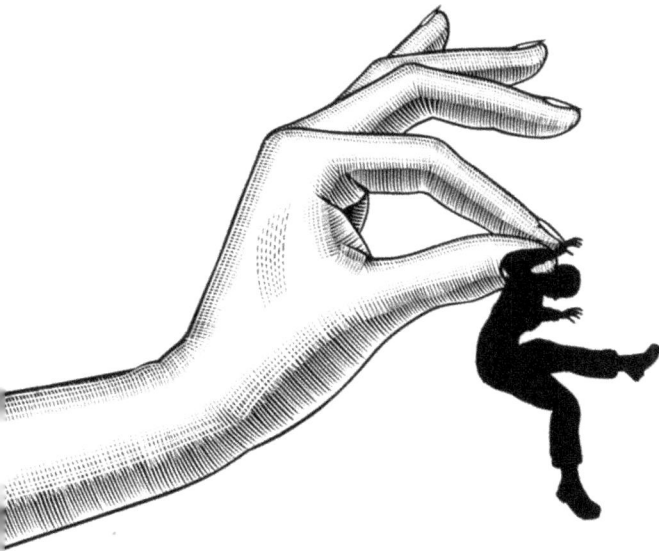

SUBMISSION (DAY 27)

/səb mish' en/ *The instance of giving over or yielding to the power or authority of another*

> **DAILY AFFIRMATION:** "I submerse myself in submission so that I can be made strong in Him.**"**

> **MEMORY VERSE:** *"But he said to me, 'My grace is all you need. My power is strongest when you are weak.' So, I am very happy to brag about how weak I am. Then Christ's power can rest on me."* **2 Corinthians 12:9** NIRV

HELPFUL HINTS: Wives spend so much time trying to be strong. We've become great imposters, if you will, because we believe that others need and want to view us as independent and strong. Even being known as the "weaker vessel" makes us cringe. We want people to think that we have a strong sense of style, so we shop for the latest fashions, look for the most appealing hairstyles, and decorate our homes with the most up-to-date embellishments. Sometimes we want people to think we are strong spiritually, so we pray the loudest and the longest and we quote the most scriptures. We even attempt to show this strong side to our husbands when we rebel against their plans and their ways of thinking.

Aspiring to have your own style and your own opinion is not wrong. God created us to be thinkers, innovators, and change agents. But when our inability to conform and ultimately completely surrender gets in the way of who we really are, it becomes sinful and ugly. God wants us to be genuine and to be our authentic selves. He created us with a "weak spot" on purpose. He wanted us to sell out to the fact that we could not make it without Him. He designed humans to be dependent on others and ultimately on Him. Like Paul in our memory verse, sometimes God is not going to make that change in your life that you are so ready for Him to make. That job, that situation, and that husband may not change to what or who you want, but your ability to be vulnerable and rely solely on His grace can change.

Christ is at His strongest in our lives when we are in a state of complete rest, when we can completely give our needs as wives over to Him and let Him do the work in us. Pure 100% joy, peace, and fulfillment as a wife only comes when we stop trying to be the wife we know we should be and allow God to form us into the wife He wants us to be. Letting go of the control you have is the hardest thing to do, but by holding on to it, you and your marriage pay the price of never being what God intended it to be. Are you ready to *never* be what God wants you to be?

"WHAT TO DO" IF YOU FALL OFF: We must develop a strong sense of inner self. In times today, when you find yourself being "too strong," reflect on how Christ showed meekness on the cross. His strength under control was manifest in His weakest hour as a human. If Jesus Christ was able not to flex his muscles and get off the cross for us, how much more willing should we be about our meekness in marriage?

💜 **HEART QUESTION:** How do you feel when you are put in situations where you can't move, like being in a stalled car or elevator, in a long line, or stuck sick in bed?

_____

_____

_____

_____

_____

REFLECTION: Take time in the next few days to watch or re-watch the movie _The Passion of the Christ_. Use the space below to write down how Christ showed strength under control. His meekness was often viewed as weakness. Do you agree or disagree?

_____

_____

_____

_____

_____

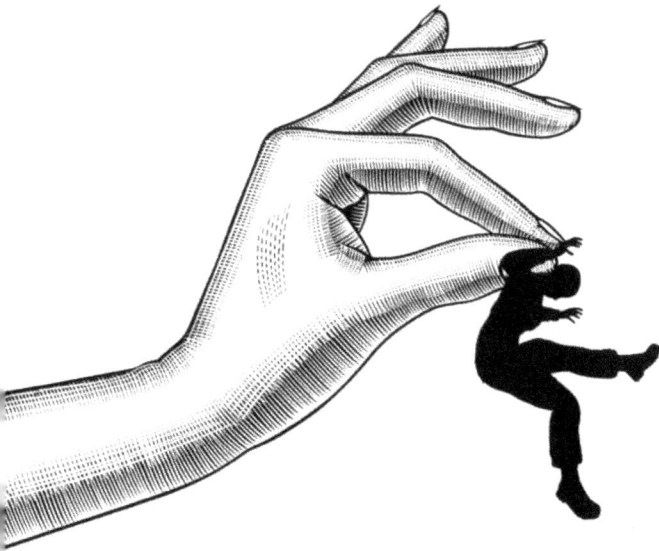

SUBMISSION (DAY 28)

/səb mish' en/ *The instance of giving over or yielding to the power or authority of another*

DAILY AFFIRMATION: "My submission toward my husband is a sacrificial act of praise."

MEMORY VERSE: *"Each of you should give what you have decided in your heart to give, not reluctantly or under compulsion, for God loves a cheerful giver."* **2 Corinthians 9:7** NIV

HELPFUL HINTS: In our memory verse today, Paul wrote to the church at Corinth to help redirect their thinking regarding giving to the church. He wanted them to recognize that if their hearts were not in giving, God was not excited about it. God would rather you give what you can with your whole heart instead of giving what you think He wants with half of it. We are not fooling

Him as wives by submitting on the surface. I am reminded of the little girl who was told by her parents to sit down several times, and when she finally obeyed, she said, "Mamma and Daddy, I may be sitting down, but I am standing up in my heart!"

God wants our submission to envelop us and be powered from our core. He wants it to be reflexive. When our husbands hit that "knee-jerk" response in us, God wants our answer to be submission. However, He does not want this from us if we can't give it with the right attitude. At this point, we ought to realize that submission is not a punishment, it's a safeguard. God always wants what's best for us; He sets up plans for us to help us, not to harm us (Jeremiah 29:11). He wants us to love what He designed for us because He knows it's best. The problem is we don't. We think we know best and have the right plan and the right map to get to what we want, and so we forego the blessings of God for the blessing fulfilling self. Ultimately, we lose, our husbands lose, and the generations that come after us lose.

When you choose to follow God's plan wholly and completely, with the right heart, you enable your children and your children's children to be set up for life. Just one act of disobedience can set the course of your family in the wrong direction. Do you want that plight on your head? When you decide in your heart that you are going to accept the gift of submission and give it with a cheerful heart, you end up giving God the ultimate form of praise. It becomes not just a thing you do on Sunday mornings in church, but a way of life.

"WHAT TO DO" IF YOU FALL OFF: Search for a picture of a lamb. Copy that picture and cut it out. Secure it to the inside of your purse, wallet, or bookbag, someplace where you know you will see it often throughout the day. Make sure that when you decide to choose rebellion instead of submission, you can see the picture of that lamb, one of the most submissive animals ever created. Refocus and remind yourself that you are that lamb.

HEART QUESTION: What does my submission look like daily? Could my husband rate it highly on a scale of 1 to 10?

_____

_____

_____

_____

_____

_____

REFLECTION: Ask your husband to rank your ability to submit on a scale of 1 to 10, with 10 being the highest. Don't get mad at the response. Instead of asking him about your score, reflect here on why the number is what it is.

_____

_____

_____

_____

_____

_____

_____

_____

_____

_____

_____

_____

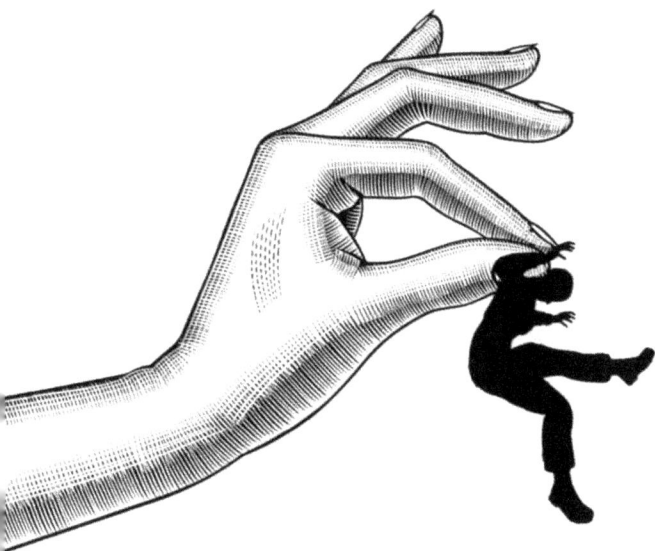

CONSISTENCY (DAY 29)

/kə́n sis' tə́n sē/ *The condition of cohering or holding together and retaining form*

DAILY AFFIRMATION: "My consistent godly behavior as a wife will bring forth miracles."

MEMORY VERSE: *"Better is the end of a thing than the beginning thereof: and the patient in spirit is better than the proud in spirit."* **Ecclesiastes 7:8** KJV

HELPFUL HINTS: I can remember watching my daughter, when she was younger, play in the snow like it was yesterday. Let me paint the picture more vividly. She was dressed in her full two-piece pink snowsuit, hat, mittens, and matching scarf. Her outfit was completed with her black waterproof snow boots with pink hearts adorning the heels. The snow drifts that

she could not wait to dive into were at least two feet taller than she was. The temperature was 11 degrees, and the sun was shining. She could not wait to tackle, jump in, climb on, and roll around in the great white, cold, fluffy stuff. Her anticipation was off the charts just looking at what she was about to dive into. After 15 minutes of absolute pleasure, she was not ready to come in. Her mittens were soaked, and I know her little hands had to be freezing. I watched all of this from the kitchen window and realized that the discomfort of her cold, wet hands did not outweigh the satisfaction and fun that was gained by playing in the snow.

As wives, we often have been neglected and mistreated so much that we forget how much pleasure our marriage or the thought of marriage once gave us. We tend to focus on the temporary discomfort instead of looking forward to the victory of a complete and full marriage. You have been working hard these last 28 days to overcome and tackle some of the toughest jobs that we have in marriage. I am confident that you have made some strides and had some victories. Don't allow the enemy now to come in and ruin all your hard work by magnifying the pain and discomfort that comes with forgiveness, obedience, trust, and submission. Play through the pain this time, and vow to be consistent in these areas of your life as well as in other areas that God has revealed to you on this journey. Your job is not over just because you've made it through these past days.

Some of you are on the brink of your breakthrough; some of you may need to repeat the steps again or maybe even a third time. Whatever God has for you and your family, don't let it be kidnapped. See the joy in playing in the snow of your marriage even though it may get cold, wet, and uncomfortable at moments. Listen, God is ready to be your comforter. He wants you to play in the freedom and safety that comes with being a wife. Are you ready to hold it together and retain your current form so that the miracle of your best marriage can break forth?

"WHAT TO DO" IF YOU FALL OFF: Get back up! Confess to your Father your fatigue about doing things His way. Find peace in the fact that He is ready to meet you where you are. Contact your accountability partner and ask for prayer specifically about continuing your life-changing journey.

HEART QUESTION: List here the most challenging area that you have had to reflect on in the past 28 days and what made it so challenging.

_____

_____

_____

_____

_____

REFLECTION: Use the space below to explain to God why, after all the work you have done, you would still consider giving up on your marriage.

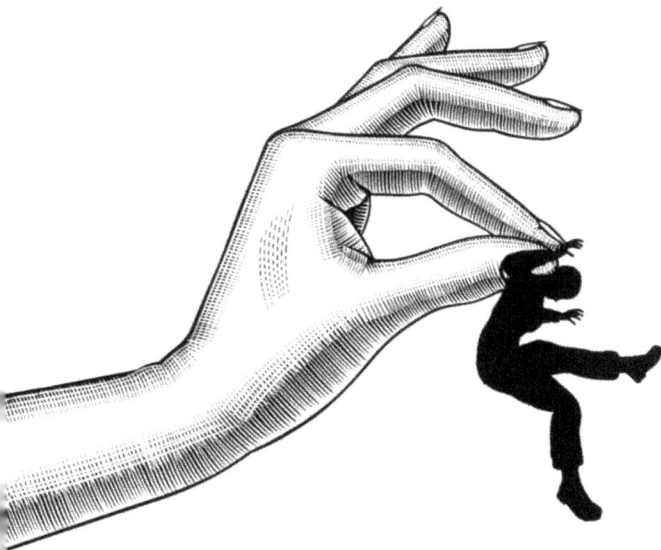

COMMITMENT (DAY 30)

/kə- mit' mə́-nt/ *To maintain a trust in a given plan of action*

DAILY AFFIRMATION: "I will stay on course and dedicated to the plans God has for my marriage."

MEMORY VERSE: *"Jesus replied, 'No one who puts his hand to the plow and looks back is fit for service in the kingdom of God.'"* **Luke 9:62** NIV

HELPFUL HINTS: So, what's a girl to do now? You have made it to the finish line, and all you need to do is cross over into the new life that God has waiting for your marriage. During these last days, you have forgiven, obeyed, trusted, and submitted like Christ. You must be walking more efficiently in the image of Christ in your marriage, and God is honoring your

faithfulness right now. He has seen your good work, and He is ready to reward you. You should recognize your accomplishments and reflect on how much you have changed. As you should have figured, this challenge was not about what God would do in him, but more about what He would do in you.

The ideal example of commitment in my mind is to be persuaded into buying a product and continuing to buy it over an extended amount of time. If you have a favorite washing detergent or cleaner, no matter how dirty, grimy, or filthy the clothes or things you are cleaning are, you are going to turn to that product. No matter how you feel about the laundry, no matter how many loads you must wash, you are going to pick that detergent. Your opinion on the product and its value does not change because of the task that you have or how you feel about the task.

That is basically how it is to be a godly wife. We made this lifetime commitment to be a wife of noble character because we have faith in His product. We know that God does not put out junk. He does not offer a money back guarantee and then renege on you. God is real and His promises are true. If He commanded us as wives to reverence and respect our husbands, then that is simply what He expects, and He has given us the tools to do it.

Our journey reminds me of the song that says, "I'm not going back, I'm moving ahead. I am here to declare to you, my past is over. In you, things are made new. I surrender my life to Christ; I'm moving, moving forward."

Believe that your ability to maintain your status as a wife is valuable to the kingdom right now and forever! You have changed generations to come by your change. Of course, there will be tests, trials, and tribulations; nothing worth having comes without a price. Decide today that what you have done in these days really does matter. You may not see miraculous changes now; you may be weary and say, "What's the point?" But at the end of the day, when you have done all that you could do, I am confident that God will do all that He can for you.

My parting words for you are from Ephesians 6:13-18 MSG: "*Be prepared. You're up against far more than you can handle on your own. Take all the help you can get, every weapon God has issued, so that when it's all over but the shouting, you'll still be on your feet. Truth, righteousness, peace, faith, and salvation are more than words. Learn how to apply them. You'll need them throughout your life. God's Word is an indispensable weapon. In the same way, prayer is essential in this ongoing warfare. Pray hard and long. Pray for your* **sisters**. *Keep your eyes open. Keep each other's spirits up so that no one falls behind or drops out.*"

"WHAT TO DO" IF YOU FALL OFF: Refuse to allow guilt and fear to set in at this point. Face it, you are going to fall; you will not be perfect in this race of wifedom. God, and no one else, has set or will set that standard for you. Each day, each hour, and each minute of your life from this point forward should

be dedicated to living as the wife you know you are to be. Take one breath at a time and live the way you have been commissioned to live.

💜 **HEART QUESTION:** What is one "thorn in your flesh" (2 Corinthians 12:7-10) that you know you will continue to struggle with as a committed wife? How will you allow God's grace to impact that thing?

_____

_____

_____

_____

_____

REFLECTION: Discuss here the most valuable lesson that you have been taught during these last 30 days. How will you continue to glean from that lesson as you go forth as a committed wife?

_____

_____

_____

_____

_____

"OKAY, SO 30 DAYS AND NOW WHAT?"

God is so good, and I believe if you have completed this 30-day challenge and held on to the principles that God has called you to as wife, then you have a testimony. To end your 30-day challenge in style, please commit at least one more week to the following:

o Journal about your journey; what did you learn most about yourself? How will this knowledge impact you as a wife?

o Please write your husband a letter indicating everything you have learned about yourself and your marriage in the last 30 days.

o   Ask him to fill out the husband survey.

o   Repeat the challenge as often as needed.

o   REJOICE, REJOICE, AND REJOICE AGAIN about all the wonderful things that God has done – He is able!

HUSBAND'S SURVEY

Please answer the following questions as accurately as possible. I grow as a wife when you share, and I have matured in the last 30 days. I can accept what you share with me in love.

Please circle your answers 1 (strongly disagree) – 5 (strongly agree)

1. Do you believe that my ability to forgive you and others has improved?

   1   2   3   4   5

2. Do you believe that my ability to obey God and sumbit to you has improved?

   1   2   3   4   5

3. Do you believe that my trust in God and our marriage has improved?

   1   2   3   4   5

4. Do you believe that my ability to submit to authority has improved?

   1   2   3   4   5

5. Do you feel that I am consistent and committed to God's Word regarding being a wife?

   1   2   3   4   5

List one thing that you feel like I do well as a wife:

_____

_____

_____

_____

_____

_____

_____

What's one thing I can still work on?

_____

_____

_____

_____

_____

_____

_____

_____

_____

_____

_____

_____

_____

Lastly, if you realized after performing this challenge that you have not accepted Christ and you would like to be become a believer, it's not too late.

Question: *If you were to die today, are you 100% sure that you will go to heaven? If your answer is no, then God designed this time perfectly for you. Please review the following:*

THE ROMAN ROAD TO SALVATION

Step 1: All Have Sinned

Romans 3:10 KJV *"As it is written, there is none righteous, no not one."*

Romans 3:23 *"For all have sinned, and come short of the glory of God."*

Step 2: There Is a Penalty for Sin

Romans 5:12 KJV *"Wherefore, as by one man sin entered into the world, and death by sin; and so, death passed upon all men, for all have sinned."*

Romans 6:23 KJV *"For the wages of sin is death, but the gift of God is eternal life through Jesus Christ our Lord."*

Step 3: God's Provision for Sinners

> Romans 5:8 KJV *"But God commendeth His love towards us, in that while we were yet sinners, Christ died for us."*

Step 4: How to Receive the Lord Jesus Christ

> Romans 10:9 KJV *"'That if ye shalt confess with thy mouth the Lord Jesus, and believe in thine heart that God hath raised Him from the dead, thou shalt be saved."*

> Romans 10:10 KJV *"For with the heart man believeth unto righteousness and with the mouth confession is made unto salvation."*

> Romans 10:13 KJV *"For whosoever shall call upon the name of the Lord shall be saved!"*

> Romans 10:14 KJV *"How then shall they call on him in whom they have not believed? And how shall they believe in Him of whom they have not heard? And how shall they hear without a preacher?"*

Step 5: Pray the Sinner's Prayer

"Lord Jesus, I confess my sins before you now. Forgive me. I believe that Jesus died on the cross and God raised Him from the dead. Save me Now Lord Jesus!"

If you believe what you just participated in is true, then you now need to find a Bible-believing institution that can share more details with you about your decision. God is really excited about your future, and so am I. I know you began this devotion seeking change in your husband, but aren't you glad to now understand that change always begins with you? Be well and enjoy your wife life!

www.ingramcontent.com/pod-product-compliance
Lightning Source LLC
Chambersburg PA
CBHW060358090426
42734CB00011B/2178